W9-BDP-150

COMPING TECHNIQUES

VISUALIZING AND PRESENTING
GRAPHIC DESIGN IDEAS

SUZANNE WEST

A READ/WRITE PRESS BOOK

WATSON-GUPTILL PUBLICATIONS

NEW YORK

A Read/Write Press book

First published in 1991 in New York by
Watson-Guptill Publications, a division of
BPI Communications, Incorporated
1515 Broadway, New York, N. Y. 10036

Library of Congress Cataloging-in-Publication Data

West, Suzanne,
            Comping techniques : visualizing
and presenting graphic design ideas / Suzanne West.
            p. cm.
            ISBN   0–8230–0767–7
            1. Computer graphics. 2. Graphic arts—
Technique. 1. Title.
T385.W477   1991
604.2—dc20   90-23725
                        CIP

Manufactured in the United States of America

First printing, 1991

1 2 3 4 5 6 7 8 9 10 / 96 95 94 93 92 91

Macintosh is a registered trademark of Apple
Computer Inc. PageMaker and Freehand are
registered trademarks of Aldus Corporation.
Pantone Matching System (PMS) is a registered
trademark of Pantone Corporation. Pixel Paint
is a registered trademark of SuperMac Corporation.
PhotoShop and Illustrator are registered trademarks of Adobe Corporation. MacPaint II is a
registered trademark of Claris Corporation.

ACKNOWLEDGMENTS

Because this book grew out of a workshop, its direction has been influenced by the hundreds of students who have participated through the years. I wish to thank these students for their questions, interests, concerns, serendipitous discoveries, and willingness to experiment. I am also indebted to the designers who so generously shared their insights, techniques, time, and examples of their work, particularly Russell Leong, Paige Johnson, Yuki Nishinaka, Ed Seubert, Renée Flower, Henry Brimmer, and Mark Anderson. I also wish to thank Paul Grosjean at Design Spectrum for his expertise and assistance with Macintosh color output, and CBM Type for their excellent image setting services.

I especially wish to thank Dorothy Spencer of Read/Write Press for her enthusiasm, encouragement, and support throughout the project; Candace Raney and Mary Suffudy of Watson-Guptill Publications for making the project possible and Carl Rosen for editing; Marisa Bulzone for her editing and insightful comments; and Penelope West, not only for her versatility as a production assistant, technical illustrator, and hand model, but also for her continued encouragement throughout the project. Finally, I wish to thank Randy Moravec, to whom this book is dedicated. Without his technical assistance, patience, generous design contributions, and endless experimentation with computer-based techniques, this book would not have been possible. His insightful and amusing observations and his dedication to quality provide continuing inspiration.

TO RANDY

CONTENTS

This book grew out of a workshop I started teaching over ten years ago, inspired by the realization that many design students receive little or no training in techniques used in creating comps. The materials, tools, and techniques introduced in the workshop have changed considerably over the past ten years. Photocopying has become more versatile and available, specialized comping materials have been introduced, and the range of services available to the designer has broadened considerably. With the introduction of the personal computer, graphic-oriented software, and laser printing, the techniques and tools used for visualizing graphic design ideas are changing even more.

In our studio, we began using Macintosh computers in 1984 to do some sketching and comping tasks, but it has only been within the past year that we have phased out conventional comping in favor of computer-based techniques. Many of the studios and agencies around us are making similar transitions. Flat files and drawing boards now sit as reminders of another era. Designing is at once more intense, more frustrating, and more satisfying. Although we feel more autonomous, we have become more dependent on technology.

New tools and techniques expand our options, but old skills (and the people who use them) do not automatically become obsolete. In design, some things, such as drawing and designing skills, are "device independent" and do not go out of style. To work visually with any medium, we must develop the ability to see details and subtleties, both of which are learned in drawing. To design, we must learn how to think about and develop ideas. The purpose of comping—to communicate an idea visually—also remains the same.

For all intents and purposes, the visualization of an idea is the idea itself; it is the only tangible evidence of the idea, and it is the primary way by which the idea is judged. It is in the designer's best interests, then, to learn good visualization skills. An attractive comp will give a good impression of an idea, whatever its intrinsic value; a poorly visualized idea may be either overlooked entirely or judged too harshly.

A comp does not only represent an idea, it also represents a printed piece. The comp cannot be thought of as an end in itself or it may lose the potential to become a printed piece, at least within the parameters of the client's budget. Part of learning to comp is learning to think of each part of the comp as having a counterpart in prepress and printing.

As the comping techniques workshop evolved, it became apparent that to know *how* to comp the student needed to learn technique; to know *what* to comp the student needed to understand prepress and printing methods; and to know *when* to comp the student needed to be familiar with the design process and procedures. Although all three topics are introduced in this book, it is not the intent to cover all three topics in depth. Rather, it provides the reader with a broad, integrated view of the visualization process used in graphic design, with a focus on technique.

This book is made up of four sections: Section 1 provides background information about the design process and prepress and printing, so the reader understands what a comp is and how it fits into the overall design process. Section 2 is an annotated list of materials and tools. Section 3 provides set-up and preparation procedures, such as creating and working with underlays, color basics, and construction and drawing techniques. Section 4 is an overview of specific sketching and comping techniques, including computer-based techniques. The appendix includes a chart of prepress and printing methods with their sketching and comping equivalents and a range of grids and type specimens to use as underlays. The 800K Macintosh-compatible disk that has been included with this book provides an assortment of files with which to experiment.

More important than any of the specific techniques introduced in this book are the strategies they embody—strategies that will enable the reader to develop new techniques and adapt to new tools. Many of the strategies and techniques used with paper translate easily to the computer screen. Learning both conventional and computer techniques gives the designer more versatility than learning only one or the other. Such versatility is important when we consider that the materials, tools, and techniques we use strongly influence the form our ideas take. By using a variety of materials, techniques, and technologies we will not confuse any one of them with creativity itself.

1

Section 1 provides the reader with the general background information necessary for developing and visualizing graphic design ideas. The design process is explained by showing how and when visualization is used in the development and presentation of a graphic design idea. Basic information is also introduced about production, prepress, and printing, the phases that follow the initial design, because most graphic designs will be printed.

VISUALIZATION FORMATS

There is no single correct way to visualize design ideas, nor is there a single technique that is appropriate for each design project. However, there are formalized ways in which designers in each field work; for example, product designers present ideas as marker sketches, whereas graphic designers generally present ideas as *comps*, or *comprehensives*. Comps are visual representations of graphic design ideas.

Within the overall category of comps are levels of refinement. A *loose comp* is a visualization that shows the general idea for a design—what elements are to be included, what sizes and shapes these elements will be, and where they will appear on the page. For clarity, loose comps are referred to as *sketches*. A *tight comp* is a visualization that provides more specific information about the design, such as type style and use of color. Whereas a sketch could never be mistaken for anything but a sketch, a tight comp could be mistaken for an actual printed piece if viewed from a distance. In this book, tight comps are referred to simply as *comps*.

CLARIFYING THE MENTAL IMAGE

A verbal description of a visual idea creates a mental image, but there is no guarantee that the image formed in the listener's mind will match that in the speaker's. To ensure that others develop the image you want them to see, you must show visual ideas in a visual form. As the saying goes, a picture is worth a thousand words.

The sketches shown here all fit the following description, but each represents a different mental image. These sketches are only a few of many possible visualizations, and all of them are "right" because there is no single correct solution to a design problem:

Visualize a black-and-white brochure that is promoting a lecture series on modern architecture. It has one fold; unfolded, it measures 8 ½-by-11 inches. On the outside of the brochure we see a photograph of part of a building; it has been screened back to create a gray texture. We also see the words *architecture today* in white on a black bar. Opening the brochure, we see the words and bar again, as well as three photographs, each of a different building. Brief text describes the theme of the series; additional text lists dates and locations of the five-lecture series.

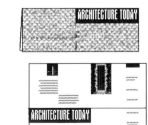

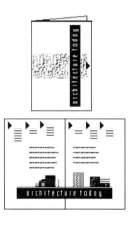

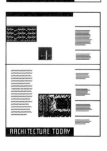

Of these hundreds of thumbnail sketches for a logo, fourteen ideas were selected for further development as sketches. Because a project of this type has an infinite number of possible solutions, the designer narrowed the range of potential design directions early in the process by choosing to design a symbol rather than a logotype.

By limiting himself to two typefaces at the beginning of the thumbnail process, the designer narrowed the range of possibilities even further. By imposing limitations of this kind, the designer could pursue a particular direction more thoroughly.
(Russell Leong Design)

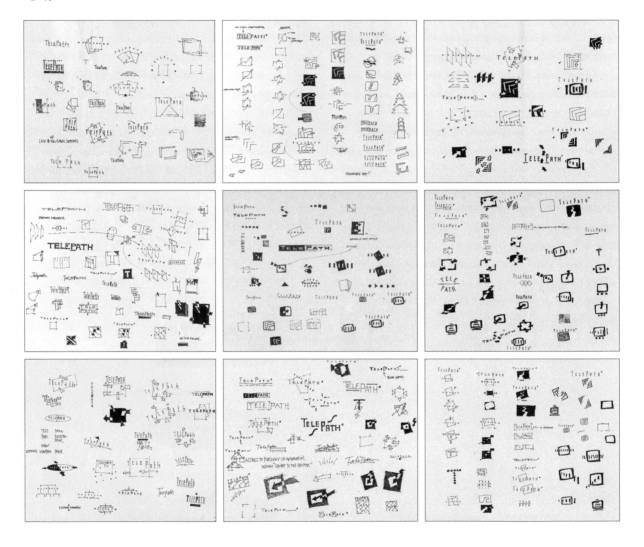

The process of design begins with visualization; visualization typically begins with thumbnails. *Thumbnails* are very small sketches that should be done relatively quickly. The small scale of the thumbnail helps the designer avoid being sidetracked by details too soon. Thumbnails are most commonly drawn simply as visual records of ideas, and they provide a visual record of the designer's thinking process. If the nature of the project offers the chance to explore a wide range of ideas, the designer may draw hundreds of thumbnails. In the development of a logo, for example, it is appropriate to explore a wide range of possibilities. Other design projects may be no more than *composition* (layout) problems—format and content may be predetermined. Once initial ideas have been recorded, thumbnails for this type of project should be drawn to the correct proportion, as inaccurate proportions can be extremely misleading. Layout thumbnails can include a considerable amount of information about the color, texture, scale, and placement of the design elements so that they provide good visual feedback.

Roughs, or full-sized, quick sketches, are typically drawn with a fat black marker or soft pencil on tracing paper; they are sometimes drawn in place of thumbnails. Roughs are only "rough" if they are done quickly and spontaneously. A skilled sketch artist can include a considerable amount of information and character in a rough. Roughs are often used in place of thumbnails and are more common in advertising than in graphic design. Roughs are more typical of the era of the commercial artist than of the graphic designer.

Blocked out layouts, in which elements are represented by boxes, help the layout artist plan how elements will fit together once a design has been established, and they have traditionally been used for the layout of newspapers and newsletters. This approach is inappropriate as a design visualization technique, because it does not show how the actual page will look.

Because the client was familiar with the imagery, and because he had a close working relationship with the designer, this rough was all the client needed to see. *(Paige Johnson Design)*

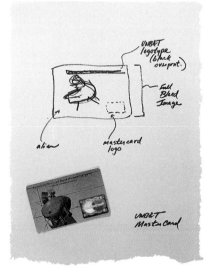

SKETCHES AND LOOSE COMPS

Sketches, by definition, are spontaneous in character. Because each person has a different set of skills and abilities, each will produce sketches that reflect these differences. A good sketch achieves a balance between control and spontaneity. A sketch that is too controlled may look forced or awkward; a sketch that is too spontaneous, however, may look sloppy or careless. In graphic design, a sketch includes elements such as typography and printing techniques, and is sometimes called a *loose comp*. For our purposes, the term *sketch* will be used to indicate both sketches and loose comps.

Sketches are typically drawn with markers or pencils on marker paper, tracing paper, or vellum, and they are generally drawn to actual size. The designer often uses such methods as underlays to increase speed and accuracy. An *underlay* is anything that is used as a tracing guide; it may include type, guidelines, graph paper, illustrations, and any other element useful to the designer.

In a sketch, elements are *indicated;* what is drawn represents specific elements such as photographs or text. An indication has the qualities of the element—color, contrast, proportion, and shape—but not the detail. Sketching, more than any other kind of visualization, requires practice. Games that require quick sketching, such as Pictionary, are extremely useful in helping to develop spontaneity and visual communication skills.

From the hundreds of thumbnails shown on page 18, only these were selected for further development. Of these, only two were refined and presented as comps. *(Russell Leong Design)*

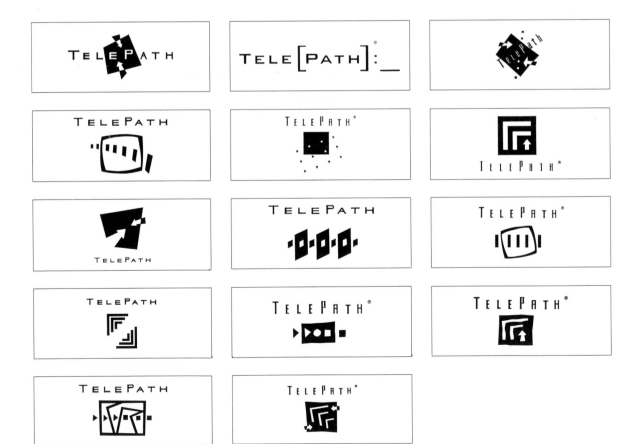

A comp, also called a *presentation* comp or *tight* comp, so accurately represents a printed piece that it could be mistaken for one from a few feet away. Comps are more formal than sketches. They are likely to be used in the following situations: when a design is being shown for the purposes of selling the design; when the client is not visually perceptive or experienced; when the project involves a significant amount of money; or when someone other than the designer will be assuming responsibility for production and printing. There are levels of refinement in comps, just as in sketches. In a highly refined comp, type is set and converted to the correct color; photographs are taken and printed to scale; and illustrations are drawn to reflect the finished product as nearly as possible. It is not unusual for people within a large studio or agency to specialize in creating these highly refined comps. On a more typical comp, the designer may use *greeking* (type set in nonsense words), *found* photographs (existing photographs that represent the photographs proposed by the designer as accurately as possible), and colored papers and films that represent final, printed color.

A number of materials and tools are manufactured specifically for comping; because a designer can produce a comp in the same amount of time it takes to produce marker sketches, comps have become a fairly standardized presentation format. Comps communicate better visually and leave less to the imagination than sketches, and they can draw the viewer's attention more to the design idea than to the designer's drawing ability.

Comps are sometimes accompanied by *dummies* or *mock-ups*, which are accurate, three-dimensional representations of the piece. In presenting a comp for a book or a catalog, for example, the designer might also show a dummy that is made to the correct trim size, with the correct paper and number of pages, and bound in the proper manner.

It would be difficult to distinguish these business card comps from printed pieces. To create comps this precise, the designer had to consider even the smallest details. If less precise comps had been created, many of these details would not be resolved until the production phase. *(Russell Leong Design)*

With the introduction of the computer as a graphic design tool, traditional distinctions between roughs, sketches, comps, and production art are being redefined. The computer may be used as a way to comp parts of a design, such as to set type that is laser printed onto comping paper, or the computer may be used to create the entire comp.

Graphic designers who work with computers can often produce a higher level of refinement more quickly than with traditional tools, but because current software has been developed for graphic production rather than graphic design, it is sometimes difficult to use the computer in the early part of the design process. The temptation is to refine too early, and precision becomes as much a curse as a blessing, forcing the designer to make detailed decisions about such specifics as type before an idea has been fully developed as a whole. To avoid this problem, designers who use computers often look at their work only in a reduced size or use simple paint programs that discourage refinement.

Working on the screen with a paint program is more like sketching; working with a layout program and printing out the results is more like creating camera-ready art for reproduction. Although a comp has the same purpose as a sketch—to communicate an idea—it is more like camera-ready art in terms of precision. Because a comp is relatively precise, the designer often finds that he or she spends more time comping but far less time creating camera-ready art after an idea has been accepted. Because the designer can quickly produce endless variations on an idea when working on a computer, many designers report that they spend more time on design than they used to but get better results.

Materials, tools, and technologies inspire, but it must be the designer's ideas that drive the process, not the tool or technology itself. In deciding how to use a computer in the design process, the purpose for each phase in that process must be kept in mind and the software should be used appropriately: thumbnails and roughs are for recording ideas and establishing some general design directions; sketches are for testing these ideas by exploring them visually in more detail; comps are created only after preliminary design thinking has taken place, showing as closely as possible what the idea will look like when produced.

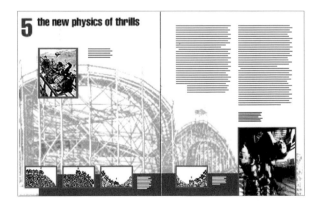

This sketch for a book design was created on a computer with a paint program, which combines the spontaneity of sketching on paper with the ability to quickly copy or modify elements.

The graphic designer, like the architect, works in an indirect medium—the materials and processes used to produce the final design are not the ones used to create the finished product. Just as the sketches and models created by an architect represent a building, so the sketches and comps created by the graphic designer represent a printed piece. Both the architect and the designer must keep this in mind throughout the design process. To predict the final product, the designer, like the architect, must understand his or her medium. Such an understanding allows the designer to use the medium to advantage—the designer can explore new ways in which to use the medium and can draw inspiration for design from the medium itself.

Once a design has been accepted, the design phase ends and the production phase begins. The designer is often the only person working on the project who is considering the design as a whole. The first part of production often involves coordinating the work produced by the vendors who are creating the elements for the design. It is the designer's task to ensure that the parts being created will fit the overall design concept and work together as planned.

The comp provides a wealth of information to vendors and such coworkers as production artists, printers, and photographers. Because it is "comprehensive," a comp can serve as a reference; it is often used to obtain accurate estimates from vendors. In studio environments where design and production are separate departments, the comp may be the only vehicle by which the designer and the production artist communicate. A trend in recent years, however, has been for designers to assume responsibility for production as well. This enables the designer to retain control of the many seemingly small decisions that so often affect the overall quality and integrity of a final printed piece.

Students developed their ideas for this assignment in thumbnail and sketch form. Because the typographic details are an integral apart of a typographic design, students set type and produced camera-ready art to use as a master for making these photocopy comps. *(Bob Raymond and Martin Venezky)*

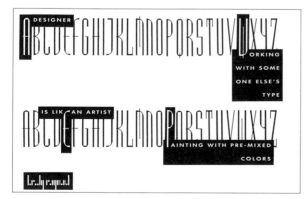

CAMERA-READY ART

Before a design can be printed it must be translated into *camera-ready art*, the photographic master from which the printed piece is created. The comp gives an impression; camera-ready art must be precise. The human eye forgives and interprets; the camera does not. The camera-ready art shows the exact sizes, shapes, and locations of all the elements in the design, as well as exact trimming and folding lines. Information on the camera-ready art must be in black or red (which is seen by the camera as black) because the process camera "sees" only as black or white. Camera-ready art is accompanied by any images, such as illustrations and photographs, that will also require processing prior to printing. Also included with the camera-ready art are specific prepress and printing instructions.

Prepress is the phase in which camera-ready art is converted into printing plates. An assortment of materials and techniques are used to transform the camera-ready art and any accompanying photographs and illustrations into printing plates. A separate plate is required for each color to be printed. The camera-ready art and other images are photographically converted to film negatives; each may require different kinds of photographic processes. Once the separate films have been created, they are *stripped* (taped) together in precise position. Often dozens of separate films must be shot and *booked* (assembled) to create a single master film for each of the printing plates required. To understand printing and production, it is necessary to understand some key prepress processes and terms, some of which are introduced on the following pages.

This camera-ready art (left) is all that was needed for this four-color book cover (right).

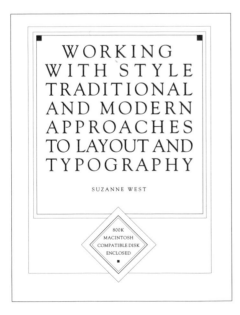
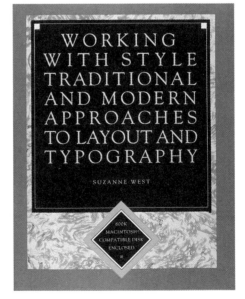

LINE SHOTS AND LINE ART

When original art is simply black and white, such as typography or pen-and-ink drawings, it is considered *line art* and can be photographed onto paper or film as *line shots*, images that have only black and white with no *intermediate values* (grays). In a line shot, the camera interprets any intermediate values on the original as either white or black. An original image with intermediate values changes considerably when shot as line art. When it is important to retain the intermediate values, the art is shot as a halftone.

HALFTONES

Halftones are black-and-white copies of *continuous tone* images (those that contain intermediate values), such as black-and-white photographs. A halftone contains no grays. Instead, it simulates the gray areas in the original with patterns of small black dots—the darker the value, the larger the dot. When we look at a halftone, our eyes blend the black dots with the white of the paper and we perceive a shade of gray.

The dots are created by *halftone screens*, which are referred to by the number of lines (rows of dots) per inch. The more dots per inch, the higher the *resolution*, and the more detail and subtlety will show in the image. In a coarse screen (*low* resolution) of 65 to 85 lines (of dots) per inch, such as those used for reproducing photographs in newspapers, the dots are so large that they are visible to the eye; minute detail is obscured. The dots of a fine screen (*high* resolution), such as those used in slick magazines, are visible only when viewed through a magnifier.

In addition to regular halftone screens, there are *special effects* screens. These are either regular patterns such as diagonal lines or concentric circles or irregular patterns such as *mezzotints* that look somewhat like coarse photographic film grain. Special effects screens are sometimes used to add texture and create interest.

A black-and-white photograph can undergo a number of transformations during the prepress process.

Line art

Mezzotint

DUOTONES

A continuous-tone image, such as a black-and-white photograph, can be converted to a *duotone*, which is a single halftone image of the photograph printed twice, one on top of the other, in two colors. A duotone is generally printed in two different colors, and one color is generally lighter than the other. In a duotone, care should be taken that the second color is appropriate for the subject; green, for example, is generally an inappropriate choice for a client portrait. A duotone printed in two shades of black, or black and a warm gray, lends an overall richness and intensity to black-and-white photographs. In a standard duotone, the light areas remain white, but a duotone effect can be produced by printing a halftone over a tint background.

TINT SCREENS

Tint screens are patterns of dots or lines in regular patterns that are used when a color is to be printed as though it had been mixed with white. The amount of white paper showing between the dots changes the *value* (lightness or darkness) we perceive; for example, red ink becomes pink, and black becomes gray. Tint screens are specified by lines (rows of dots) per inch just as halftone screens are.

The value of a tint screen is controlled by the size of the dot and is referred to by percentage: a 50 percent tint screen produces a medium value, while a 5 percent tint screen produces a very light value. On a specific tint screen resolution (e.g., 85-line screen) only the size of the dot changes, not its position, so a 90 percent tint of an 85-line screen uses the same pattern of dots as a 10 percent tint of an 85-line screen. The dots appear closer together because they are larger. Tint screens are most commonly available in 10 percent increments and are sometimes available in 5 percent increments as well. When more than one color is being printed, tint screens of different colors can be printed to mix colors (see *Color Theory* in section 3).

100-line-per-inch photographic halftone

COLOR SEPARATIONS

Color separations are made from continuous-tone color images through a filtering system in which the process camera "sees" only one color in the image at a time. Color separations rely on *four-color process* theory, which states that any color can be matched by mixing only four colors: *magenta* (a shade of red), *cyan* (a shade of blue), *yellow*, and *black* (see *Printing in Color* in this section, and *Color Theory* in section 4).

Today, color separations are controlled to some extent by computers. An image, generally a *transparency* (a photograph printed on film, such as a 35mm slide), is scanned to separate the color. In scanning, the computer translates an image into a form that can be stored digitally. Once an image has been scanned, some computer systems allow extensive manipulation of the image, including many of the tasks previously done by photo-retouching artists using airbrushes. Such tasks might include removing unwanted elements from an image, changing colors, applying textures and patterns, and seamlessly combining elements from more than one image.

DIGITAL PREPRESS

When a computer is used to create black-and-white camera-ready art, the file must be printed onto *repro* paper (light-sensitive, high-contrast photographic paper) by an output device, such as a Linotronic image setter. Linotronic output can also be a *film positive* (black image on clear), a *film negative* (clear image on black), or a printing plate. When the output is on paper, it is used in the prepress process like any other camera-ready art. When the output is on film, some prepress work is eliminated. When the output is a printing plate, no prepress is needed (or indeed is possible). Given the speed at which digital prepress technology is advancing, personal computers will be an integral part of the prepress process by the time today's graphic design students are out of school.

100-line-per-inch digital halftone

Commercial paper is available in two broad weight classifications, *text* and *cover,* and in two types of finishes, *coated* and *uncoated.* Both text and cover stock come in a variety of weights in each type of finish. Uncoated papers are often textured and are available in a number of colors; coated papers are seldom textured and are most often available only in shades of white. Coated papers may be either *glossy* or *dull.* Most are coated on both sides (*C2S*), but some cover stock may be coated only on one side (*C1S*).

Cast-coated paper is extra glossy because its clay-coated surface is heated and pressed against a smooth chrome drum during manufacture. It is usually coated on only one side. The coating on paper acts as a barrier between the ink and the paper fibers. Paper fibers absorb printing ink, so an image printed on uncoated paper is not quite as crisp and bright as the same image printed on coated paper. Color printing is most commonly on coated stock because the hard surface allows finer detail.

Commercial papers can generally be purchased only in large quantities for printing and are seldom available in retail stores. The papers available in retail stores are typically not available in quantities for commercial printing. Paper is generally purchased by the printer in *parent* sheets (large sheets of paper in standardized sizes), which are sized to accommodate a final 8 ½-by-11-inch page size.

Paper has a *grain* (a specific direction in which the paper fibers lie) that must be considered when designing folded pieces. Folding against the grain cracks the paper along the fold, producing a ragged edge. Although most printers consider grain when ordering paper for a job, the designer should also consider grain when designing a job for a specific size of parent sheet.

SAMPLES

Because commercial paper is not commonly available in art supply stores, it is often difficult for the designer to know what papers are available or how to specify them. Most paper manufacturers make paper selectors and swatchbooks for their products; they and their distributors usually will send these out on request. Many paper manufacturers also advertise their new papers in design magazines and generally provide a coupon for ordering a swatchbook. Swatchbooks provide invaluable information about a paper's colors and weights, parent sheet sizes, and grain direction. Because some of these specifications change periodically, it is wise to replace swatchbooks yearly and to confirm the availability of papers with the printer or the paper distributor before including a specific paper in a comp.

Although anything you comp can be printed when cost is no factor, it is likely that you will be working within a specific budget and time frame. Therefore, a basic understanding of printing is an essential part of achieving a printed piece that matches your design. There are a number of printing technologies; each has its own capabilities and limitations. To comp for a specific type of printing, one must be aware of these capabilities and limitations.

OFFSET LITHOGRAPHY

Because almost all printing today is offset lithography, the term *printing* generally refers to this method. A key advantage of offset printing is its ability to print fine detail very precisely. Another advantage is that once a press is set up to run, large quantities can be printed relatively quickly; the larger the quantity, the lower the cost per piece (*unit cost*).

In offset lithography, a flexible metal plate is wrapped around a drum. On the plate is emulsion in the shape of the image to be printed. Only the emulsion area accepts printing ink—areas without emulsion are wetted to repel the ink. The plate is inked, the inked image is transferred (*offset*) to a rubber *blanket*, and the blanket is pressed against the paper running through the press. The color that appears on the paper is determined by the color of the ink that is applied to the plate.

A separate printing plate is required for each color to be printed during a single press run. A printing plate could be used to print a different color during another press run.

Offset printing presses are referred to by the number of colors that can be printed as a sheet of paper goes through the press; a *one-color* press has a place for only one printing plate; a *six-color* press has positions for six printing plates in sequence. A sheet of paper printed with six colors on one side may have passed through a one-color press six times, a two-color press three times, or a six-color press once. If the paper had passed through a one-color press six times, the printer would have needed to clean and set up the press six times. If the paper had passed through a six-color press, however, the press would only have been set up once. If the paper passed through a one-color press six times, one would not know exactly how the printed piece would look until the final color had run, whereas if a six-color press were used, the designer would see the results at once and could order subtle adjustments to be made during printing.

Offset presses that print on sheets of paper are called *sheet-fed*; offset presses that print on a continuous roll of paper are called *web-fed*. Except in print shops with small presses that can only print on 8½-by-11-inch paper, most sheet-fed printers print on parent sheets. Often several images of the same piece are printed side by side and then cut apart; small brochures can be printed in one pass through the press. Most sheet-fed presses print on one side of the paper at a time. Most web presses are *perfecting presses*, which print on both sides of the paper at once. These are costly to set up and are generally used for very large jobs, such as books, or for very large quantities of a small piece, such as a catalog.

LETTERPRESS PRINTING

The *letterpress* is the most traditional type of printing press; the principle of letterpress printing has not changed for hundreds of years. On a letterpress, a raised surface is inked and then pressed against the paper. Originally, woodcut illustrations and hand-set metal type were the kinds of elements that were printed. Today, any camera-ready art can be photographically converted into a zinc plate with a raised surface. Letterpress printing is seldom used for commercial printing anymore, but it is sometimes used for other processes, such as die cutting and embossing. The art of letterpress printing is kept alive primarily by printers who print limited-edition books. Letterpresses run more slowly than offset presses and are more labor intensive, so the unit cost does not drop as dramatically when printing large quantities as it would with offset lithography.

SCREEN PRINTING

In *screen* printing (often erroneously called *silkscreen* printing), a stencil of a design is affixed to a mesh screen, usually made of polyester or metal. The stencil is most commonly created photographically from camera-ready art. A separate screen is made (*burned*) for each color. Ink is pressed through the mesh of the screen onto the printing surface with a squeegee. Commercial screen printing is typically used for binder covers, plastic packaging, t-shirts, product labels, signs, and posters. Screen printing cannot reproduce the same fine detail as offset lithography; the size of the mesh determines the amount of detail possible. Despite advances in screen printing technology, it remains a labor-intensive process and the cost per piece does not drop significantly when large quantities are printed.

This title page from a limited-edition book is typical of those produced with hand-set type and letterpress printing.

EMBOSSING, DEBOSSING, AND STAMPING

Embossing is a term used for the process of deforming the paper surface into a raised design. (When the process deforms the paper surface into a recessed design it is called *debossing*.) Seals on certificates are often embossed, as are logos on business cards.

Embossing requires a *die* (mold) in the exact shape to be embossed. The most common and least expensive die is a *magnesium* die, which is created photographically from camera-ready art. A *brass* die is used for more complex embossings and when large quantities are embossed. Brass dies are engraved by hand and may have combinations of surfaces, textures, and edges. An embossing die is a recessed form; the printer makes a corresponding raised form from a plastic material. When the paper goes through the press, the raised form presses the paper into the recessed die with sufficient pressure and heat to permanently stretch and deform the paper. (Common terminology in the trade still refers to the recessed die as *female*, and the raised form as *male*.)

If the paper is left unprinted in the embossed area, it is called a *blind* embossing. Some change in the color and texture of the paper generally occurs during the embossing process, and this effect can be increased if the designer so desires. For more contrast, the paper is sometimes preprinted in the same shape as the embossing die; this is called a *register* embossing because the printing and the embossing must align (register).

A thin layer of foil can be placed between the paper and the embossing die so that during embossing the foil is fused onto the paper in the shape of the die; this is called a *foil embossing*. Foil is available in a variety of colors and finishes, most of which do not look metallic. Foils can be transparent or opaque, shiny or dull.

Foil stamping is similar to foil embossing. It requires a metal die in the shape of the design, but the die only flattens the paper as the foil is fused onto the paper, and the paper fibers are not stretched or deformed.

Nothing on this piece is printed. All of the color is foil that has been stamped, embossed, or debossed.

VARNISHES AND COATINGS

Large areas of color printed on coated papers are generally protected either by a varnish or a plastic coating. Varnishes are applied like ink and can be used in place of ink in the last color position on a multiple-color press. Varnishes can be glossy or dull, clear or tinted. A *tinted* varnish is one to which a very small quantity of ink color has been added.

When a varnish is applied as the last color on the press, with the ink still wet, it is a *wet-trap* varnish. When the varnish is applied in a separate run, after the ink has dried, it is a *dry-trap* varnish. Dry-trap varnishes are generally more expensive because they require a separate press set-up, but they tend to produce a more even surface. Varnish can be applied overall or in spots. An *overall* varnish does not require a printing plate—the varnish simply coats the entire surface of the paper. A *spot* varnish is applied only to designated areas and requires a printing plate just as an ink color would. Varnishes are referred to by their surface and amount of coverage—for example, *OAGV* means an overall gloss varnish.

Coatings are most often glossy *UV* (ultraviolet) coatings and are generally applied overall as a separate operation. Coatings look similar to dry-trap varnishes but provide more protection. They tend to be used on products that are handled frequently, such as book and report covers.

DIE CUTTING

Any printed piece that is not cut at right angles in a single cut with a paper cutter must be cut with a die. The most common kind of die is a *steel-rule* die, which is a strip of steel cut and bent into the desired shape. A steel-rule die works much like a cookie cutter: its sharp metal edge is pressed against the paper and cuts the paper to shape. Folded boxes, presentation folders with flaps, and tabbed dividers in binders all require die cutting. Special shapes such as triangles are also die cut, even though they have straight edges that could be cut with a commercial paper cutter.

BINDING

Traditional, *sewn* binding is still used for high-quality, hard-cover books, but *saddle stitching* is the most common binding for brochures and booklets. After the pages are collated and folded, staples are put through the fold to hold them together.

Perfect binding is the method used to hold paperback books together. Pages are assembled, then glued to make the spine. Printed pieces that are saddle stitched or perfect bound are printed on oversized paper (parent sheets), assembled, bound, and then trimmed so that the edges of the pages align perfectly.

Mechanical bindings are commonly used for technical documents, reports, and instructional materials. Plastic-comb binding, wire-comb binding, spiral binding, and three-ring binders are examples of mechanical binding; in each, the inside edges of the paper are punched and the binding is visible on every page.

Printing ink is thick and sticky; when applied to paper, however, it becomes a thin, transparent layer. Because of the ink's transparency, most color is printed on white paper. When ink is printed on colored paper, the color of the paper alters the color of the ink. Often what we perceive as colored paper is, in fact, white paper that has been completely covered with ink. Printing color on white paper gives us a wider range of hues and values—there are many more colors of printing inks than there are colors of paper. When matching ink colors, however, we must be aware of the many different shades of white paper, because even relatively subtle differences in whiteness will affect the color we see when it is printed.

COLOR-MATCHED INKS

There are two fundamentally different approaches to color printing. The most direct way is to mix printing inks in the colors we want and then print them on the paper. A standard reference for mixing ink colors is the Pantone Matching System (PMS)*, a set of specific mixing formulas. To specify a color, the designer needs only to refer to the color by number. A good reference for Pantone colors is a swatchbook; the best version to use is the *PMS Color Formula Guide*, which includes the mixing formulas. Pantone markets a number of comping materials and supplies that are intended to match Pantone ink colors (see section 2).

FOUR-COLOR PROCESS PRINTING

The second approach to color printing, *four-color process* printing, is based on the principle of *optical simultaneity*, in which the eye blends together whatever colors it sees at the same time. This is how all of the subtle and diverse colors in a color photograph can be reproduced without needing to make a plate to print each color individually. In four-color process printing, only process ink colors—magenta, cyan, yellow, and black—are put on the press. Process colors are seldom printed as pure solids because they are "raw" colors and tend to be harsh. Instead, solid areas of color are produced by overlapping tint screens of two or more process colors. Photographs are reproduced by being *separated* (the process in which a separate halftone is created for each process color). We can reproduce the color photograph by printing each halftone on top of one another to recombine the colors as dots (see *Prepress* in this section, and *Color Theory* in section 3).

Although we can print an almost infinite number of colors in color photographs, we are limited in the colors we print with tint screens because they are available only in fixed increments of 5 or 10 percent. To match some colors, including many Pantone colors, we would need tint screens in other percentages as well. Pantone makes special percentages of tint screens for matching their colors with four-color process printing, but not all printers stock them.

Because computerized prepress capabilities are becoming more sophisticated, however, it should be possible in the near future to match virtually any color using the four-color process system.

2

2

Section 2 is an overview of the materials, tools, and supplies commonly used to create sketches and comps of graphic design ideas. It is divided into five parts. The first, *Basic Tools and Materials,* is an overview of the tools and materials that will be of general use, whether you sketch, comp, or use a computer to sketch or comp. The second, *Sketching Tools and Materials,* lists the materials and tools that are most useful for creating sketches of ideas. The third, *Comping Tools and Materials,* focuses on those materials developed specifically for comping graphic design ideas for printed pieces. The last two, *Equipment* and *Computer Tools,* introduce basic equipment as it is relevant to design, rather than to business or production. At the end of this section is a summary of the materials and tools listed in each part plus a list of the typical services a designer buys from vendors.

STOCKING YOUR TOOLBOX

The materials and tools described in this section are intended as a point of departure for stocking your toolbox. Buying materials and supplies is an ongoing process—do not expect to purchase everything you will need at once. Plan to experiment with a wide range of products to discover the materials and tools best suited to your particular range of skills and projects.

Over the years, designers collect a hodgepodge of tools, supplies, and materials; most will tell you that they use only a portion of what they have, yet they will continue to try many of the new products that are introduced each year. Some of these new products will be improvements on what the designer is currently using; others will offer new capabilities. Large art supply stores often give demonstrations of new products, and some stores will let you test these products yourself.

Materials and supplies vary widely in cost; experiment freely with those that are relatively inexpensive, but shop carefully before investing in more expensive tools and supplies. Before investing in equipment, think about your particular needs and research what other designers are using. Often, instructors, employers, or peers will recommend products that they find useful. It is generally a good idea to buy products that are recommended rather than buy what seem to be less expensive products. Many bargain products do not provide the same capabilities, nor do they function as well.

TESTING BEFORE YOU BUY

Whenever possible, test the materials and supplies before you buy them (see *Testing Procedures* in section 3). Ask about a store's return policy on graphic art supplies before you purchase anything, especially on products that cannot be tested in the store. Occasionally a material or tool you buy is faulty, and you will need to exchange it for another—make sure you have the option of returning bad products. Occasionally a new product will not perform as advertised. You want the option of returning these products as well. If you are buying a product that is unfamiliar to you, however, ask about its use before you buy it and make sure you follow directions carefully.

THE ISSUE OF TOXICITY

Only in recent years has there been an awareness of and concern about toxicity in the materials and supplies used in graphics. Many instructors and designers who have been working in the field for a long time do not think of the supplies they use as toxic and may not consider toxicity as a problem. For your own protection, use common sense and always read and obey the warnings and instructions that accompany the supplies you use. Some supplies may not include warning labels; for example, most solvents and adhesives come with warning labels, but many markers do not. Do not automatically assume that a product is nontoxic simply because it does not have a warning. As a general precaution when using any inks, paints, and solvents, avoid excessive skin contact, keep them away from your eyes, and work in a well-ventilated area to avoid fumes and airborne particles. Always stop using a product if you notice an adverse reaction to it.

The basic materials and tools described here will be useful for general graphic design work, whether you are sketching, comping, or using a computer for most of your design. Although some brand names have been included for reference, get in the habit of evaluating and testing materials on your own.

PAPERS

—TRACING PAPER is thin, translucent paper that is available in pads, rolls, and loose sheets; it comes in a wide variety of sizes. Tracing paper has a hard, toothy surface that accepts colored pencil well and resists penetration by markers. Relatively inexpensive, tracing paper is widely used for thumbnails, roughs, and sketches. Most designers keep a 9-by-12-inch tracing pad handy for sketching, even if they work with a computer for most of their design. Most tracing paper works well with most markers, but the way in which tracing paper accepts marker varies from brand to brand, so test before you buy.

—MARKER PAPER is whiter and less translucent than tracing paper. Its absorbent surface accepts colored marker and colored pencil well. Because marker paper is relatively opaque and absorbent, colors appear more intense than on tracing paper, but because of its opacity it is not as easy to use with underlays unless you have a lightbox.

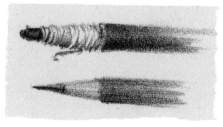

SKETCHING TOOLS

—BLACK MARKERS are available in several *nib* (tip) shapes and sizes, and it is useful to have a variety of these on hand. Black markers vary widely in the shade and density of black they produce, and the density and color they produce varies with the type of paper on which they are used. Experiment to see which combinations produce the best results for you. *Chisel-tipped* markers are broad and flat so that you can draw either wide or thin strokes, but they are most useful for wide strokes and for filling in large areas. Stabilo, Prismacolor, and Pantone all make good quality chisel-tipped markers. *Bullet-head* markers have a fat round point; a popular and widely available brand is Sharpie. *Fine-tipped* markers, such as those made by Pilot, are available in several nib thicknesses.

—COLORED MARKERS. Fine-tipped colored markers come in a variety of nib sizes and are useful for adding color to thumbnail sketches, as well as for adding color accents to comps. A small set of fine-tipped markers, such as those made by Pentel or Buffalo, offers basic colors, but it is often more useful to purchase markers separately to get only the colors you want. Pantone and Prismacolor also offer a range of chisel-tipped markers. These tend to be considerably more expensive than other brands of markers, but each comes in both fine- and chisel-tips, so marker colors may coordinate better than markers purchased piece meal.

—GRAPHITE PENCILS. A mechanical pencil with .05mm lead (*graphite*) will make predictable thin lines, but some people still prefer conventional wood-and-graphite pencils. If you like to use a pencil for sketching, you will want to have an array of graphite drawing pencils with soft and medium-soft leads; you will also need an eraser that is soft enough to avoid roughing up the paper surface.

—BLACK DRAWING PENCILS, such as Prismacolor or Derwent Studio pencils, offer more contrast than graphite pencils, which actually draw in gray, not black. Black pencils combine well with black markers to provide a good range of detail and texture. Black, paper-wrapped wax pencils called *china markers* are also useful.

—ERASERS are relatively inexpensive and a wide range is available. You may wish to try several types because different combinations of papers and pencils will require different erasers. White plastic erasers such as MagicRub tend to be the most versatile.

STRAIGHTEDGES, SCALES, AND RULERS

A *straightedge* is a true edge that is used as a guide for drawing and cutting straight lines; it need not have measurements on it. A *scale* is a measurement device that may or may not also be a straightedge. A *ruler* is a combination straightedge and scale that allows you to draw and cut straight lines as well as to measure.

—STEEL STRAIGHTEDGES are made of steel, a metal that is hard enough to resist nicking when used as a cutting guide. Because steel is heavy, these straightedges also help hold work in position; however, steel straightedges over 24 inches in length are cumbersome to work with.

—CLEAR PLASTIC RULERS. Several manufacturers make clear plastic rulers; some of these have a metal edge so that they can be used for cutting as well as drawing. C-Thru makes an inexpensive line of metal-edged rulers that are accurate enough for most comps and come with either pica or inch scales printed on them.

—PLASTIC TRIANGLES are available in both clear and transparent colors; they come in a wide range of sizes and prices. Colored triangles are the most useful because they are easier to locate on a table full of paper. Most designers have at least two basic triangles: a 45° triangle and a 30°/60° triangle.

—A T-SQUARE is a straightedge with a perpendicular piece (T) fastened to one end. When it is aligned with a true edge on a drawing board, the t-square allows you to draw and cut parallel lines.

—A PARALLEL RULE is a sliding straightedge that is fastened to a drawing board at both ends. Many people find a parallel rule faster and more accurate to use than a t-square. Mayline parallel rules have been a popular standard for decades, and several styles are available, both with and without drawing boards. Because quality varies widely between styles and brands, plan to invest in a sturdy parallel rule. If you choose to buy one already mounted on a drawing board, test it to make sure that it slides smoothly and easily.

—SCALES in both picas and inches are necessary for most graphic design work. A traditional metal typesetter's scale, or *pica stick*, has both inches and picas and is accurate enough for most sketches and comps. Precision Rules, manufactured by Schaedler, are extremely accurate scales made of flexible, frosted plastic; there are a number of other flexible scales on the market.

CUTTING TOOLS

—ART KNIVES. The most common art knife used by graphic designers, the X-acto knife with a #11 blade, has been a standard in the graphics field for decades. It is commonly available not only in art supply stores, but also in stationery stores and hobby shops. Refill blades are also easy to obtain. You should plan to replace blades frequently so that cuts are crisp and clean.

—CUTTING MATS are sheets of hard plastic coated with a softer plastic that "heals" when it is cut. Surfaces such as chipboard and illustration board cut easily, and the grooves left by old cuts can deflect your knife blade when you make new cuts. Cutting mats come in a variety of sizes. (Cutting mats also make excellent mouse pads for your computer.)

BASIC EQUIPMENT

—DRAWING BOARD. It is not necessary to have a drawing board for sketching—any reasonably flat surface will do. A portable drawing board with a t-square, or a drawing board with a parallel rule attached to it, however, will help you work more accurately when doing comps. Drawing boards are available with or without parallel rules. Parallel rules can be attached to most drawing boards, but check with your art supply store to make sure that the drawing board you are buying will be appropriate for mounting a parallel rule. Many designers prefer a portable drawing board on a desk or table to a free-standing drawing board, and portable drawing boards are considerably less expensive. A drawing board should be large enough to hold a 15-by-20-inch sheet of mounting board.

—LAMP. A lamp that can be easily repositioned is essential. The most common variety is a drafting lamp that clamps onto the edge of a drawing board or table, such as those made by Luxo. A lamp with both incandescent and fluorescent lighting gives more natural light and better color balance than either incandescent or fluorescent alone.

—LIGHTBOX. There are many inexpensive lightboxes on the market today, ranging in size from 4-by-5 to 24-by-36 inches in surface area. Choose a lightbox that can be lifted with one hand so that it is easy to move in and out of your work area. Avoid lightboxes that have a raised lip around the edge because they are difficult to use with a t-square. A lightweight lightbox, however, will probably not have a glass top, so buy an inexpensive sheet of clear plastic thick enough to resist cutting to lay on top of the lightbox. C-Thru makes plastic sheets with red grids printed on them that are ideal; the grid also helps you align elements quickly.

TAPES, ADHESIVES, AND SOLVENTS

—WHITE PAPER TAPE or *drafting tape* is useful for holding work in position. Because they have a relatively high-tack adhesive, however, they are too strong to use on many of the delicate paper surfaces used in comps.

—MAGIC PLUS TAPE by 3M is a translucent tape with a low-tack adhesive similar to the adhesive on 3M's Post-it brand notes. It is safe to use on the delicate paper surfaces used in comps to hold pieces in position temporarily, and it works well as a *frisket*, or mask.

—SPRAYMOUNT by 3M is a repositionable spray-on adhesive that neither shows through tracing paper, discolors it, nor causes it to buckle when it is lightly applied. Because this adhesive can be applied evenly, it can even be used on the back of clear acetate to hold it in position. SprayMount is fast and easy to use, but like other aerosols it should be used in a well-ventilated area.

—RUBBER CEMENT is widely used for production art; it is a reasonable alternative to SprayMount for those who do not want to use an aerosol. However, it stains some paper surfaces used in comps. Other adhesives that are useful in different applications, such as paste, wax, and glue sticks, are not useful for comps either because they warp the paper, do not hold securely enough, or do not apply evenly.

—BESTINE is a brand name for an alcohol-based solvent sold as a thinner for rubber cement. It removes adhesive residue and fingerprints from a comp without discoloring delicate paper surfaces. (In England, lighter fluid is used for the same purpose.) All solvents and chemicals should be used in a well-ventilated area, and you should avoid getting them on your skin.

OTHER SUPPLIES

—WHITE ACRYLIC paint or designer *gouache* (opaque watercolor paint) is useful for adding small white details, such as reversed type, to sketches. White-out can also be used for this purpose.

—A DESK BRUSH or a large, soft paint brush is useful for dusting off paper surfaces and removing small particles from the drawing board and the paper on which you are working. A wooden-handled Japanese brush with soft white bristles works well; horsehair desk brushes are made especially for this purpose. You will also need a fine brush for occasional detail work. A good quality pointed sable brush with a round ferrule is recommended.

—MAGNIFIER. A magnifier, also called a *lupe* or *linen tester*, is useful when you want to analyze how a piece was printed. At a magnification of about 800 percent, you can clearly see the dots of halftones and tint screens.

—LINT-FREE WIPES and cotton swabs are convenient for use with Bestine for cleaning off comping surfaces, as well as for cleaning accumulated pencil, ink, marker, and adhesive from tools.

COLOR REFERENCES

Printed colors change with age and with exposure to light; colors printed on different materials may match in one kind of light and look quite different in another. Do not expect exact colors to match exactly; use swatchbooks and color specimen books as a general reference only. Plan to update all color references regularly.

—PANTONE SWATCHBOOKS show all of the Pantone ink colors available; the *Color Formula Guide* swatchbook contains mixing formulas as well. All are useful as reference when comparing colors or mixing paint for a comp.

—PROCESS COLOR REFERENCES. A number of books show combinations of process color tints. These may not be accurate enough for specifying color on camera-ready art but are useful for visual reference when deciding on colors for a comp.

OTHER REFERENCES

—TYPE SPECIMENS. Although some commercial typesetters provide their customers with type specimen books for tracing and reference during comping, it is more likely that you will need to purchase a specimen book from an art supply or bookstore. Choose a book that has a good range of sizes from which to work. (Some type specimens are included in the appendix.) With a computer and a laser printer, you can make specimen sheets of the typefaces on your system.

—PREPRESS AND PRINTING REFERENCE. A brief overview of prepress and printing terms is included in section 1 for reference. A number of books on the market provide more in-depth information on this subject; many of these also include instructions and tips on how to prepare camera-ready art. *Pocket Pal* is a standard, handy reference for production information and is available in many graphic art supply stores. It was first published by International Paper decades ago and is periodically updated to keep pace with changes in technology.

—MAGAZINES. Design publications are good reference for new tools and materials. *How* and *Step-by-Step* show techniques and procedures for sketching and comping.

The materials and tools listed here are those that you will need for creating sketches of your ideas. Most of these materials and tools are convenient to have on hand but some should be purchased only as needed (see the *Comparison Chart* in this section).

PAPERS

—VELLUM is similar to tracing paper, but it is thicker, crisper, and considerably more expensive than tracing paper. Vellum has an even texture and translucency and should not be confused with *parchment* paper, which has a blotchy look meant to suggest the parchment used in old documents. Available in pads in an assortment of sizes, vellum is suitable whenever a sketch needs to look more refined.

—LEDGER PAPER is a coverweight paper, similar to two-ply bristol board, and is available in pads with either a *plate* (smooth) or *vellum* (toothy) finish. Sketches drawn on tracing paper or vellum are sometimes trimmed and mounted on ledger paper for presentation.

MARKERS, PENS, AND PENCILS

—COLORED MARKERS. Before investing in a large set of expensive markers, buy a few of several brands in an assortment of colors and work with them to see which is the most compatible with your sketching style and the paper you want to work on. Markers are either water-based or solvent-based; each has its disadvantages. Water-based markers tend to wet the paper and disturb the paper surface when multiple layers are drawn; solvent-based markers should be used in a well-ventilated area.

Berol Prismacolor markers, Eberhard Faber Design markers, and Pantone markers all offer an extensive range of colors and come in a variety of tip sizes. Pantone markers are numbered to match the colors in the Pantone Matching System (PMS), but do not expect the markers to match the colors in the PMS swatchbooks exactly. Pantone also makes sets of markers that represent the equivalent of tint screens in a limited range of colors, including process colors. Stabilo makes a line of chisel-tipped, water-based markers in a wide range of colors.

Pentel and Buffalo both make inexpensive sets of water-based, thin-nibbed markers that are useful for sketching thumbnails and adding small areas of color. These are a good supplement to the brands of designer markers already mentioned, not a substitute.

—BRUSH PENS offer the convenience of a marker with the flexibility of a brush. There are several brands on the market, but the range of colors is limited. Pentel's refillable brush pens have a more flexible tip than other brands, which have relatively rigid tips that are more similar to markers than brushes.

—MARKER SPRAY DEVICES, or *marker sprayers*, such as the Letrajet by Pantone and the Designaire by Eberhard Faber, allow you to attach a marker to a can of compressed air to simulate airbrushing. (An *airbrush* is a painting device with a trigger that lets you control both the pressure of the air passing through the nozzle and the width of the spray area. It is connected to a tank of compressed air or to an air compressor.) Marker sprayers do not offer the same amount of control as airbrushes but are faster to use; colors are changed by inserting a different marker, so no washing up is required as with airbrushes. Marker sprayers enable you to quickly spray a small area with color or blend marker colors on the page, but they are not useful for painting large areas.

—BLENDING MARKERS are markers containing a transparent solvent that blends and lightens the marker color already applied to a page. Because they contain solvents, blending markers should be used only in well-ventilated areas. They also dissolve toner from photocopies and laser prints and can be used to transfer an image from one surface to another.

—DRAFTING PENS, such as Rapidographs, were created for technical illustrations, but are sometimes useful for adding fine detail in sketches. Drafting pens are available in a range of tip sizes and are refillable with specially made ink. Drafting pens must be cleaned regularly to keep the ink flowing smoothly. The availability of inexpensive fine-tipped black and colored markers has made the drafting pen obsolete for most sketching.

—COLORED PENCILS. Only colored pencils that lay down an even color and come in a good range of colors are appropriate for design sketching; this eliminates the inexpensive sets made for children and hobbyists. Berol Prismacolor pencils have been a favorite of designers for many years; Derwent Studio pencils are excellent for sketching as well. Each is sold both in sets and individually. A word of caution: Berol and Derwent both make other lines of colored pencils, which have different characteristics from those mentioned.

—PENCIL SHARPENERS. If you work with pencils you need a good pencil sharpener—one that works quickly and is sharp enough to point the pencil without cracking the lead. Electric pencil sharpeners and battery-operated pencil sharpeners work well; a high-quality crank pencil sharpener is also a good alternative. For portability and simplicity, however, consider the basic metal pencil sharpener with holes for three sizes of pencil made by Koh-I-Noor.

—DRAWING COMPASS. For drawing circles, buy a multipurpose compass that locks into position, draws at least a 10-inch circle, and holds a variety of pens and pencils. Many inexpensive compasses satisfy these requirements; a basic drawing compass need not be expensive.

SOFTWARE

Bit-map software, such as a basic paint program, is the computer equivalent of sketching tools and materials. Most, if not all, computers with graphic capabilities have some kind of paint program available. Paint programs are appropriate for sketching because they prevent the designer from getting too involved in details and precision; they are the most similar to sketching with markers. On a black-and-white system such as a Macintosh SE, a typical paint program is MacPaint. On a color system such as a Macintosh II, color software such as Pixel Paint enables the designer to work with the equivalent of colored markers and colored pencils (see *Computer Equipment* in this section).

The tools and materials made especially for creating comps help the graphic designer create more refined visualizations of printed pieces. Most are relatively easy to use, enabling the designer to work more quickly, but what is saved in time is often spent on materials, which tend to be considerably more expensive than the materials used in sketching. With these specialized comping materials, however, the designer can create presentation-level comps that could not otherwise be achieved. Because the presentation of an idea is so closely linked to the idea itself, most designers want to present their ideas in the best form possible.

PANTONE PAPER AND FILM PRODUCTS

A wide range of papers and films, marketed under the Pantone brand, are made especially for comping and coordinate with the Pantone Matching System (PMS) printing ink colors. Pantone introduces new papers and films periodically in response to trends in graphic design. Although Pantone papers and films are relatively expensive, the cost is generally justified by the quality. Part of what we pay for is the convenience of having a reliable, color-coordinated system of materials that corresponds to printing ink colors.

—UNCOATED PAPER has a solid PMS color printed on one side and comes in 20-by-26-inch sheets. It represents an area of color printed on uncoated white paper. Uncoated paper is available in all PMS colors.

—COATED PAPER has a solid PMS color printed on one side and a self-adhesive back. It is available in 20-by-26-inch sheets, and represents an area of color printed on cast-coated paper or on glossy, coated stock that has been gloss varnished. It is available in many, but not all, PMS colors.

—GRADUATED-TONE PAPERS AND FILMS give the appearance of being airbrushed and have such an even gradation from 100 to 5 percent color that they can be used for scanning and as camera-ready art. They are available in a limited range of PMS colors in both coated and uncoated paper surfaces, as well as on adhesive-backed film.

—COLOR OVERLAY FILM is an adhesive-backed film that is sold in 20-by-26-inch sheets; it is available in many PMS colors. Overlay films represent printing on coated stock but do not have a high gloss. Color overlay film is also available in sheets of tint screens, four tints per sheet, as well as in graduated colors. Color overlay film has an advantage over paper in that it is very thin and its edges do not show when it is applied to the comp. The strong adhesive sometimes tears the delicate paper surfaces on the comp, however, so color overlay film must be used with care. Any adhesive film must be applied carefully so that air does not get trapped under the film; air bubbles appear as discolorations and imperfections on the comp.

—PANTONE SELECTORS. Not all Pantone products are available in all PMS colors. Pantone makes selectors for most of their paper and film products; these are generally available for reference at the counters of retail stores. If you order materials by phone or mail, however, it is useful to have selectors for the materials you use most frequently so that you get a quick overview of what is available and can compare subtle differences in color between products. (Pantone also makes charts showing which materials are available in what colors.)

—OTHER PMS REFERENCES. Pantone makes a number of color guides that show tints, provide tear-out swatches, and offer other color information. (The PMS *Color Formula Guide* swatchbook is an invaluable reference—see *Basic Tools and Materials* in this section.) Pantone is a Letraset product, and Pantone materials are described in detail in the Letraset catalog, available at most graphic art supply stores. The catalog includes a section on how to use some of the Pantone products.

OTHER PAPERS AND FILMS

—COLOR-AID and CHROMARAMA are colored papers with an evenly applied color on one side. Both come in a wide range of colors that may or may not have PMS equivalents. Both are appropriate for indicating screen printing, but they may be misleading as large color areas on comps because normal offset inks may not be able to duplicate the intensity of the colors offered. They are useful, however, for accent color. Both Color-Aid and ChromaRama are available by the sheet, but color packets that contain a small sheet of each color may be more useful.

—ZIPATONE, a brand of adhesive-backed film that has been around for decades, is available both in color and with printed patterns. Zipatone is available in many art supply stores in a variety of colors, and in both matte or gloss finishes. PMS equivalents may be found for some Zipatone colors.

—CAST-COATED PAPER is cover stock with a clay coating; it has an extremely smooth, shiny surface. Cast-coated paper is almost always available with a coating on only one side; it is generally available only in white. A similar cover stock is available in colors which may or may not have PMS equivalents. Art supply stores almost always stock some brand of cast-coated paper; one of the most common brands used commercially is Kromekote, and this brand has become almost synonymous with cast-coated paper.

—TREATED ACETATE is a clear film with a clear coating on both sides that allows it to accept water-based media such as paint and ink without beading. Treated acetate looks exactly like clear, untreated acetate. Both are available in pads or by the sheet.

—MOUNTING BOARD is a high-grade, rigid cardboard that has a laminated paper surface. Comps are usually mounted on either gray or black, and there are several brands of board in these colors that are made especially for mounting graphic design comps. Letraset makes a black mounting board that has a black core; both sides are black and devoid of any brand name or logo. Mat board, used in fine art framing, is another option. Mounting board comes precut in the standard presentation size of 15-by-20-inch sheets, as well as in 20-by-30-inch and full 30-by-40-inch sheets.

—COVER STOCK is heavy paper that is typically used for the covers of brochures. Uncoated cover stock is available in a wide range of colors and textures. Coated cover stock is generally only available in white. When presenting comps mounted on board, it is customary to cut a piece of uncoated cover stock and attach it as a cover flap to protect the comp as well as to prevent the client from seeing it prematurely. Some brands of mounting board have matching cover stock.

—SAMPLE SHEETS of commercial papers were once readily available from paper distributors, but this free service is being discontinued in many areas. If your paper distributor will not provide you with sample sheets for comping, either for free or at a reasonable cost, your printer can order them for you. Sample sheets may also be available directly from a paper manufacturer. When actual paper samples are not available, match the color as closely as possible with another paper and include a paper swatch of the commercial paper you intend to use.

—PREPRINTED ADHESIVE-BACKED FILMS are made by many of the same manufacturers that make transfer materials. These films are usually patterns and dot screens, and they are more suitable for presentation graphics and architectural drawings than for graphic design comps. Preprinted dot screens are coarser than the screens actually used in printing and should not be used to indicate tint screens. To indicate the optical change in color that will be achieved with a tint screen, show the final color itself; for example, a 50 percent tint screen printed in black will be seen as gray on the printed piece, so use gray on the comp, not a dot pattern.

—FRISKETS are water-resistant or waterproof films that usually have a low-tack adhesive backing. Friskets are cut to shape and work much like stencils, masking areas that are not to receive paint. Their primary use is for masking areas for airbrushing. Frisk Film is a frisket with a low-tack adhesive that is ideal for use in comping, and it comes in either a matte or a glossy surface. This type of frisket can also be used over photo indications to indicate spot gloss or matte varnishing.

TRANSFER MATERIALS

Rub-offs, or *transfer* materials, are made of a waxy substance printed on the back of a clear or frosted plastic sheet. When it is positioned on a surface and rubbed lightly, a transfer element such as a letter is released from the plastic sheet and adheres to the surface below it. Transfer materials are made by a number of manufacturers of a variety of items, the most common of which is transfer type.

—DISPLAY TYPE, type that is 14 points and over, is typically used for headlines and titles and is available by typeface in *character sets* (upper- and lowercase alphabets, punctuation, and numbers). Letraset is a common brand of transfer type that offers a wide selection of typefaces and sizes. Letraset adds typefaces periodically in response to design trends. All of Letraset's typefaces are available in black, some are available in white, and a few are available in basic colors. Although transfer lettering comes in text and display sizes, text sizes are impractical for indicating blocks of text.

—TRANSFER TEXT looks like typeset columns of nonsense words and is often called *greeking*. Letraset makes transfer text in a limited range of sizes, leadings, and typefaces; many are available in both black and white. Because transfer text is somewhat delicate, it tends to have a shorter shelf life. (Transfer text should not be confused with text that is printed on adhesive-backed film. This film is relatively invisible when applied to white paper but is distracting on comps with colored backgrounds.)

—WORD POSITIONING SYSTEM. This Letraset product consists of a sponge, tray, and film/paper strip sets. It allows you to transfer letters to a strip of paper, re-transfer the letters to a film strip, then precisely position the letters onto a comp. The advantage with this system is that spacing and position can be previewed before the letters are placed on the comp. You do not need to purchase the entire system, although the sponge and tray are handy; the film/paper sets are sold as refills and will work as well with an ordinary sponge on a clean flat surface. Film/paper sets are available in sheets as well as strips. When the Word Positioning System is used with white or lightly colored type, the type can be colored with a marker sprayer before it is transferred to the film.

PAINT AND PAINTING TOOLS

Paint is used to indicate white type, light type, or line work on a darker background. It is not used for large areas on a comp because comping papers are not intended for water-based media. Paint can be mixed to match PMS colors (see *Mixing PMS Colors* in section 3). To apply paint, you will need either a small pointed brush or a ruling pen; to mix paint, you will need an inexpensive medium-sized soft brush.

—GOUACHE is an opaque watercolor paint that offers good consistency and opacity. It is available in many colors.

—ACRYLIC PAINT has a polymer base and works with water just as gouache does. A popular painting medium, it is commonly available in a wide variety of colors. Acrylics work much like gouache except that they do not rewet; that is, once they have dried they cannot be turned back into paint with water. This means that it is easy to paint one detail over another without smearing the first color. Gouache and acrylics can be mixed on a comp, so you can supplement the colors you want from one with colors from the other.

—CASEIN works much like acrylic paint, in that one color can be painted over another without rewetting. Casein is usually available in jars; Plaka is a common brand.

MECHANICAL TOOLS

—RULING COMPASS. If you work with paint you will need a compass that includes a ruling pen tip. Many designers have several compasses, each of which satisfies a different need.

—CUTTING COMPASS. To cut accurate circles you will need a compass that holds an art knife and locks into position so that it will not slip with the pressure of cutting. Although some inexpensive children's compasses work well for this, avoid those that have a point protector—they will not allow you to hold the art knife at a low enough cutting angle. Some companies, such as X-acto, make compasses especially designed to hold an art knife. Griffhold and several other manufacturers make a cutting blade that fits into the lead holder of a standard compass. These cutting tips work very well but, like all blades, need to be replaced frequently. To cut circles one-inch or less in diameter, you may need to use one of these cutting tips.

—DRAWING TEMPLATES are intended as drawing guides for technical drawing, but many are useful for comps as well. Circle templates and french curves are particularly useful. *French curves* have a variety of *compound curves* (curves made by combining arcs of different circumferences) to choose from.

—FLEXIBLE CURVE GUIDES are snake-like lengths of rubbery plastic that have soft metal wire inside. Flexible curve guides can be coaxed into a desired shape and then will hold that shape so that it can be used as a guide for cutting and drawing. Some are more flexible than others; they come in several lengths.

—RULING PENS were originally designed for technical inking; used with ink they take considerable practice to master, but they are much easier to use with paint. Ruling pens allow you to draw thin, light lines on dark paper. Because the tip is adjustable, you can draw lines of varying thicknesses. Ruling pens have a wide price range; an inexpensive one (under $5) is usually sufficient. If you cannot test it in the store, which is likely, run your finger along the tip to make sure it is smooth. Paint should be cleaned out of the ruling pen immediately after use; this can be done with a pipe cleaner or a cotton swab.

OTHER TOOLS

—BURNISHERS are pen-like tools with a small, hard tip at one end for rubbing, or burnishing. Burnishers are most commonly used for transfer materials but can also be used as embossing tools (see section 3 for embossing procedures). Wooden sculpting tools come in a variety of shapes and make excellent burnishers. Letraset makes a black, spoon-shaped burnisher that is useful for a variety of applications.

—BRUSHES. In addition to the desk brush and small pointed brush listed under *Basic Materials and Tools*, you may want a medium-sized soft brush with a round ferrule if you will be using paint and a ruling pen. This will be used for mixing the paint and loading the pen.

—PROPORTIONAL SCALES are wheel-like devices that show you quickly and easily what size something will be when enlarged or reduced and what percentage must be used to reach that size. Proportional scales are quick, but they are not particularly accurate. Check for accuracy before you buy a proportional scale by aligning the zeros and checking to see if the hash marks by the other numbers align as well. Even if your proportional scale is inaccurate, it may still be accurate enough for comps; do not rely on it, however, for production specifications.

—CALCULATORS are useful for arithmetic tasks such as adding up characters and lines in a manuscript and also can be used in place of a proportional scale to find percentage enlargements and reductions (see section 3 for calculating scale).

—STAPLERS are necessary for saddle-stitching. Make sure the stapler will open flat so that it can be used as a *tacker* (the points stay straight). Most desk staplers have this feature. If you will be doing a lot of saddle-stitching, you may wish to buy a long-necked stapler made especially for this purpose.

—COLOR TAG is a heat-and-foil system by Letraset for ironing plastic foil onto photocopied or laser-printed shapes. The foils come in a limited range of colors; the ones that work well consistently are the metallic colors. The paper surface used must be smooth, and the toner from the photocopier or laser printer must be dense enough to form a bond when the foil and heat are applied, but not so dense that powder is on seemingly blank areas. When all the conditions are right, this product is excellent for indicating metallic foil on a comp, but anticipate some trial and error and purchase materials accordingly.

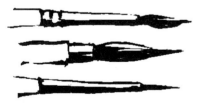

TAPES AND ADHESIVES

—DOUBLE-SIDED TAPE has a pressure-sensitive adhesive with a strong, permanent bond. It is useful in assembling packaging comps and other items with tabs that glue. There are several brands on the market, all of which are good; each has a slightly different adhesive.

—BLACK PHOTOGRAPHIC TAPE is a dull black crepe tape similar to drafting tape. It is often useful for holding cover flaps or acetate overlays in place on black boards.

—DOUBLE-SIDED ADHESIVE SHEETS are much like double-sided tape and have a peel-away protective covering on each side to keep the adhesive fresh. Sheets can be cut to the size needed and sometimes provide a good alternative to spray adhesive. Most have a core of thin plastic film that has an adhesive on both sides, but some have only the adhesive itself between the peel-away coverings.

STORAGE

—TAPE DISPENSERS keep your tape edges from collecting dust and lint. If you purchase tape in small rolls it usually comes with a tape dispenser. If you purchase the more economical large rolls, however, you will want to either keep them in their boxes or put them in dispensers.

—FLAT STORAGE. If you do not have a flat file, you will need at least one large flat container in which to store papers and board and a designated place in which it can lie flat. Always store papers flat rather than on end. Papers stored vertically will bend and will be difficult to use; board stored vertically will warp and then cannot be used for presentation.

—LARGE ENVELOPES are convenient for storing comping papers and films that come in large sheets. Available from many art supply stores, envelopes must be large enough to hold 20-by-26-inch sheets. If envelopes this size are not available, buy inexpensive cardboard portfolios or make folders by taping two sheets of railroad board or tag board together on three sides.

OUTSIDE SERVICES

—CUSTOM TRANSFERS. Although some studios buy the equipment necessary to make their own custom transfers, most designers buy custom transfers from their typesetter or graphic arts service as needed. Custom transfers can be made from any black-and-white camera-ready art. The camera-ready art is converted to a film negative, which is used to expose light-sensitive material, and color is added. Many custom transfers can be ordered as transparent or opaque in any PMS color. If you prefer, the color image can be put directly on your comping surface rather than be made into a transfer.

—PHOTOSTATS, or *stats*, are black-and-white images on paper that are created photographically in any size (within the range of paper sizes available) from any black-and-white camera-ready line art. Good quality photocopies may work as well as stats on comps. *Reverses* are stats in which the black and the white areas have been reversed, that is, the black area on the camera-ready art is white and vice versa.

—FILM POSITIVES are shot like stats but are on clear film, that is, the clear area on the film matches the white of the camera-ready art. *Film negatives* are like reverses except that they are on clear film instead of paper. Film negatives are often used as masters for creating custom transfers. Both film positives and film negatives are sometimes used as overlays on comps. Traditionally, a film negative had to be made first in order to make a film positive, because film materials were *negative-acting*, that is, they would reverse the blacks and the whites. Newer film materials can be either negative- or positive-acting, which means that a film positive can be made directly from art. This makes them more affordable for use in comping.

—COLOR STATS are created photographically from color images and are a good compromise in cost and quality between a color photocopy and a color photograph. They are a service of many graphic arts vendors but are not available in all areas.

—PHOTOCOPIES can be either black-and-white or color. High-quality, black-and-white photocopies have clean whites and dense, solid blacks. Photocopiers are not precision tools; anticipate that copies may be one or two percent larger in size than the original and that the proportions of an image may be stretched slightly. For comps, photocopies may be good enough to use in place of stats.

—COLOR PHOTOCOPIES can be made from 35mm slides as well as from printed color images. Not only can color images be copied, but black-and-white images can be copied in a color (the black is replaced by a color you select). The color on photocopies tends to be more saturated than the color on the original, so subtleties are often lost. Because the color shifts are somewhat unpredictable, it is wise to test the colors before copying. Because most copiers today are *plain paper* copiers, you can photocopy onto most text-weight stock, including uncoated Pantone paper.

—TYPESETTING can be ordered from a commercial typesetter. Many typesetters can set type *in position* to match your layout and can output the type on either paper or film. Many typesetters also offer other services, such as custom transfers. There is considerable variation in quality from typesetter to typesetter. Some desktop publishers also offer typesetting as a service; there is even more variation in the quality they provide, so ask to see samples first.

—LASER PRINTING AND LINOTRONIC OUTPUT. See *Service Bureaus* under *Computer Tools* in this section.

—SCRAP FILES. Illustrators commonly have a *morgue*, or scrap file, in which they save photographs for reference when drawing. These can be photographs of people, products, settings, flora and fauna—anything that may be useful for visual reference. Designers also often keep such a collection, which can be used as underlays or for reference in creating photo indications. Many designers also find it useful to save examples of text— different leadings, typefaces, point sizes, line lengths, paragraph treatments—as well as examples of color and layouts that might prove inspirational in the future. Other designers' scrap files contain variations on a particular kind of printed piece—catalogs, product brochures, presentation folders—and samples of different kinds of printing techniques and papers. Such samples as these are invaluable when discussing a job with a printing representative. To be useful, scrap files must be organized by subject.

—TYPE SPECIMENS. Type specimen books that have been produced using the same typesetting technology you will be using for camera-ready art are the best references. If you are setting most of your own type, you can create specimen sheets showing your available range of typefaces with different leadings, point sizes, line lengths, and justifications. You may also want to have on hand a current list of the typefaces that can be purchased for your computer system.

—PAPER SWATCHBOOKS are generally available from paper distributors and manufacturers and include such information as colors, parent sheet sizes, grain direction, weights, and availability (see *Paper* in section 1). Many paper companies advertise new papers in graphic design magazines and list who to contact for free swatchbooks. If you are on the mailing list of a design organization, you may receive swatchbooks and paper promotions in the mail.

—VENDOR CAPABILITIES BROCHURES. Printers, typesetters, and other vendors often have brochures that describe their specialties and the other services they have available. A printer, for example, may specialize in four-color or web printing and have extensive in-house prepress facilities; some may also have color separation capabilities; some have specialized binding, folding, and finishing. Knowing the capabilities of the vendors at hand can help you expand your design horizons to take advantage of these capabilities.

—PRICE LISTS AND CATALOGS. Most graphic arts services, copy centers, service bureaus, typesetters, and art supply stores have price lists. A price list not only gives you the cost of items so you can budget a project, but also a summary of what is available from each vendor. A typesetter, for example, may do much more than set type; many offer Linotronic output, custom color transfers, and photostats. Catalogs from art supply stores and mail-order art suppliers can introduce you to products you did not know existed; some offer discount prices on supplies.

—PRINTER ESTIMATE FORMS. Many printers have an estimate form for their printing representatives to fill out when bidding on a job. Such a form is a comprehensive list of all the things the printer will need to consider for the job. The estimate form is a useful checklist for looking at the comp through the printer's eyes.

SOFTWARE

There is as great a difference between sketching and comping software as between other sketching and comping tools and materials. This is because a comp tends to require more precision than a sketch.

—DRAWING SOFTWARE such as Adobe Illustrator and Aldus Freehand allows the designer to create complex shapes, to mechanically scale and space elements in a design, and to refine logos and symbols. With drawing software and a scanner, the designer can often trace a rough sketch done outside the computer, as well as a sketch done in a bit-map program.

—LAYOUT SOFTWARE such as Aldus PageMaker and Quark XPress enables the designer to create realistic layouts, as well as to integrate images created with other software into layouts. Because drawing and layout software were developed as production rather than design tools, they encourage the designer to work very precisely. Many designers find that they are working at production-level precision even before a final design has been established. This can be counterproductive, as it may encourage the designer to move out of the design phase and into the production phase before it is appropriate to do so (see section 4; see also *Computer Tools* in this section).

Equipment refers to devices beyond the basic tools used by graphic designers. Most equipment is expensive; fortunately, most of it can either be leased or is available for use through service centers. Some equipment, such as that used to make custom color transfers, may require the use of chemicals, and this might be impractical in the graphic design studio. Some equipment, such as photocopiers, may vary widely in price and features; what will satisfy comping needs may be in an upper price range. The amount of equipment you need depends a great deal on what is readily available in your area. The equipment available to you will influence how you work.

AUTO-TRACE EQUIPMENT

Light-and-lens systems that project an image onto paper for tracing have been used for decades. A traditional system is the "lucy," a vertical system of pulleys that moves the original to be traced closer or farther from the designer's tracing paper. Some auto-trace devices project images directly onto a drawing board. Unless you invest in an expensive system, lens quality is poor and the maximum size of the original that can be used is severely limited. Photocopying has effectively replaced this type of equipment for graphic designers.

FAX MACHINES

Facsimile, or *fax*, machines, enable the designer to send a black-and-white copy from one place to another via the telephone lines. For situations in which the proverbial picture is worth a thousand words, a fax machine can help simplify communication. For some projects and situations it is expedient to submit a fax of sketches or proposals before a meeting so that the client has time to review it. Some designers have reported that client meetings have been eliminated for some projects because layouts can be approved by fax.

PHOTOCOPIERS

A black-and-white photocopier is extremely useful for sketching and comping. The ideal photocopier for graphic design has a zoom lens that enlarges and reduces in one percent increments, produces dense black areas, copies onto 11-by-17-inch paper, and has a straight paper path so that relatively heavy cover stock can be fed through it. Because a photocopier with these features represents a significant investment and a service contract to keep it running, many freelance designers and small studios find that the range of services and equipment available in self-serve copy centers is more practical. Larger copy centers often provide a number of other services as well, including collating, cutting, folding, mechanical binding, and saddle-stitching.

CAMERAS

—A 35MM CAMERA and a range of lenses can be useful when developing a comp, even when the designer's photographic experience is minimal, because looking through a camera helps the designer visualize the photographic elements in a design more effectively. It also helps the designer appreciate the services and skills of a commercial photographer. Slides produced with a 35mm camera are relatively inexpensive and can be copied with a color photocopier for use in comps.

—AN INSTANT CAMERA such as a Polaroid is helpful in converting a three-dimensional object or person into a two-dimensional image. Once the photo has been made, it can be used as an underlay, photocopied to a different size for tracing and photo indication, or scanned for use in a computer-generated layout.

Computers are becoming more and more common tools for basic typesetting, drawing, and layout tasks. They are useful tools for visualizing ideas as well as for production tasks and can be used for creating sketches and comps. In using computers, designers must learn not only new ways of doing things, but also a new set of terms.

TERMINOLOGY

When we speak of computers in relation to graphic design, we are referring to *personal* computers (PCs) that are self-contained, desktop-sized machines. The other end of the spectrum is the industry-sized *mainframe* computer, in which the *CPU* (central processing unit) is shared by a number of workers who gain access to it through a *terminal* (a screen and an input device such as a keyboard) or a *workstation* (a "smart" terminal that has an auxiliary computer in it). Some workstations now have graphic capabilities.

Hardware refers to any equipment that is part of or relates to a computer. Hardware on a basic computer system consists of the computer, a keyboard, a *monitor* (screen), and a disk drive.

Peripherals are pieces of hardware such as printers and scanners that link to the basic system but are not an essential part of it.

Input devices include peripherals such as graphic tablets and scanners that allow you to put information into the computer. A keyboard is the most common input device.

Output devices are peripherals such as printers that allow you to get information from the computer.

Software refers to packaged *programs* (sets of instructions written in a language the computer understands) that allow a user to interact (*interface*) with the computer. A software product may also be referred to as an *application*, short for application software.

Software does not *interface* ("talk") directly with the computer but through a second level of program called an *operating system*. Some computers are designed to use several operating systems; others, such as a basic Apple Macintosh, have a *transparent* operating system, that is, one that is built into the computer so that the user is not aware of it. This helps make a computer *user friendly* (easy for a computer novice to use).

Software is *hardware specific*, that is, it is developed for a specific computer system. A program written for an IBM PC, for example, will not work on an Apple Macintosh, but it might work on a computer that is IBM PC *compatible*, that is, the hardware has been designed to function exactly like an IBM PC.

For graphics, a basic computer system must include not only the basic CPU (computer) but *input* devices such as a keyboard and a mouse; a *monitor* (screen) for visual feedback; a disk drive for *loading* (putting in) and *downloading* (taking out) *files* (information stored as electronic data); and a *hard drive* on which to store programs and large files.

—A MONITOR looks much like a television screen and is comprised of about 72 *pixels* (picture elements) per inch, which corresponds to the number of points per inch, the measuring system for typography. Monitors are available in color as well as black and white.

—HARD DRIVES. Many designers add an *external* hard drive as a peripheral. This provides additional storage for files and programs; some designers carry this hard disk to meetings instead of sketches and comps and present their work on the screen. (The client, of course, must have a matching computer system.)

—A MODEM is a device that allows computers in different locations to exchange information over the telephone lines. Many service bureaus accept jobs for output via modem, and the modem may be a good way for the client or writer to send manuscript copy to the designer.

—A SCANNER is a device that translates an image's pattern of light and dark into a corresponding *bit map* (an image created by dots) that can be manipulated and modified on the computer. Designers who comp on the computer find it extremely useful to scan images from the "real" world. Bit maps may be used as *templates* (guides) in a drawing program for tracing, or they be enhanced and modified with bit-map software such as PhotoShop or Studio/8 (see *Software* in this section). Photographs can be scanned into the computer for layout purposes and later included in camera-ready art as *FPOs* ("for position only" images that act as guides for scaling and positioning the actual photographs).

—A FLAT-BED SCANNER is one in which the image to be scanned is placed face down on a glass surface, much as an original is placed on a photocopier. Flat-bed scanners can produce either low- or high-resolution images. *Resolution* is the number of dots (bits) per inch; the more dots per inch (*dpi*), the higher the resolution. Flat-bed scanners can be used with *OCR* (optical character recognition) software to read pages of manuscript into the computer so that a manuscript need not be retyped. Although this system is not error-proof, it saves hours of *keyboarding* (typing).

—VIDEO TRANSLATION hardware-and-software packages such as MacVision enable the designer to connect a computer to a video camera (the camera is usually sold separately) so that anything the video camera sees can be *captured* as low-resolution, bit-map images. This type of system is useful for scanning three-dimensional products, such as packages, for use as photo indications.

—LASER PRINTERS print with the same kind of toner system found in photocopiers. A laser printout is often the only way the designer can see an accurate representation of a drawing or layout, because the image that appears on the screen has a significantly lower resolution. For comping on the computer, a laser printer is invaluable, particularly if it is compatible with *PostScript*, a graphic-oriented computer language developed by Adobe Systems. Most laser printers have a resolution of about 300 dpi.

—IMAGE SETTERS such as the Linotronic 100, 300, and 500, print on high-contrast photographic paper at resolutions as high as 2500 dpi. They output on paper, film positives, and film negatives; some are set up to output directly onto printing plates.

—COMPUTER-BASED TYPEFACES. Laser printers have computers inside them. Although most printers include a basic selection of typefaces, additional typefaces *(downloadable fonts)* can be purchased separately and installed in a computer system. Most designers build a basic library of the typefaces they use most frequently in their work. The typefaces available from companies such as Adobe and Bitstream are professional quality and, in capable hands, can be used to achieve the same level of quality produced by commercial typesetting equipment.

SOFTWARE

To work effectively, you probably will need four types of software: *word processing, paint, drawing,* and *layout*. There is some overlap between these categories; for example, layout software may include some drawing and word processing capabilities (see sections 4 and 5).

—WORD PROCESSING software is used to type text and to edit; it is patterned after the typewriter, and its basic functions are relatively easy to learn. Graphic designers tend to need only the text-editing features of this software, many of which are now included in layout programs. More elaborate word processing packages include limited layout capabilities and are often used by desktop publishers for layout, but the typesetting controls offered are not sophisticated enough for graphic design applications.

—PAINT software is bit-map oriented and allows the user to change each pixel on the computer screen individually. Because it is relatively spontaneous, a basic paint program can be used as a sketching and thumbnail tool. Like other sketching tools, however, a paint program is not a precision drawing tool. Images created in a paint program retain screen resolution no matter what kind of printer is used for output. A basic black-and-white paint program for the Macintosh is MacPaint. Pixel Paint and PhotoShop are useful if you have a color Macintosh system, not only because they allow you to sketch in color, but also because they allow you to retouch and modify high-resolution scans.

—DRAWING software is *object*-oriented. Although what you see on the screen is represented by pixels, your drawing is stored in the computer as specific objects, each of which has a specific set of characteristics that can be changed or modified. When you draw a circle on the screen in a paint program, it becomes simply a pattern of bits—it is no longer an object called "circle." When you draw a circle in a drawing program, however, the circle appears as a bit-map image on the screen, but the software remembers it as an object. Images created in a drawing program assume the resolution of the printer, so more refined images are possible than with paint programs. The most accurate and versatile drawing software on the market today, such as Adobe Illustrator and Aldus Freehand, are PostScript-based and are available on the Macintosh and the IBM PC. Drawing programs are complex, precision tools whose primary purpose is for technical illustration, but they are useful for creating elements to use in your comps and for more advanced phases of form development, such as logos, symbols, and icons.

—PAGE LAYOUT software is also object-oriented and, as the name implies, is designed primarily for laying out pages for printing. Page layout software is also an *integration* tool, that is, it allows the user to combine files created in other types of software, such as paint and drawing programs. Aldus PageMaker and Quark XPress are two of the more popular and versatile software packages currently available, and they are considerably different. In their current form, PageMaker is generally considered more flexible, allowing rapid and spontaneous changes during design; Quark XPress is respected for its precision controls. Some designers use both, but most designers choose to use the one that best suits his or her particular way of working. Both are updated frequently, and new features are added with each update. As with most major software packages, low-cost upgrades to new versions of the software are offered to current users.

The first circle (top) is an object-oriented image that takes on the resolution of the printer. The second circle (bottom) is a bit map that keeps the resolution of the screen on which it was drawn.

TRAINING

Many people purchase computer equipment without realizing that the learning curve is steep. The designer who intends to use software for his or her professional work must consider training as a part of the initial investment in time and money when buying a computer system and software. In addition to learning basic procedures for saving and organizing data, the designer will need to learn enough skills to use basic software for his or her design.

Some people learn best when locked in a room with a computer and an instruction manual; others find it useful to take short courses. In choosing a training course, look for one that is geared to your particular needs, for example, one that is taught by a graphic designer rather than by a desktop publisher or software expert. This will help ensure that you learn appropriate information and procedures for the kind of work you will be doing.

BUYING COMPUTER EQUIPMENT

A computer may be sold *bundled* or *unbundled*. A bundled system includes everything you need; for example, a Macintosh SE includes the screen, disk drive, and keyboard; some include hard disks as well. Some bundled systems even include basic software to get you started. Although this may seem to be a convenient way to buy your first computer, it is unlikely that a system that is powerful and versatile enough for graphic design will be sold bundled. Instead, you will need to order the exact combination of hardware and software for your particular kind of work. Choose a major brand, such as an Apple Macintosh or an IBM PC, so that you will be assured of a wide selection of graphic software and upgrades.

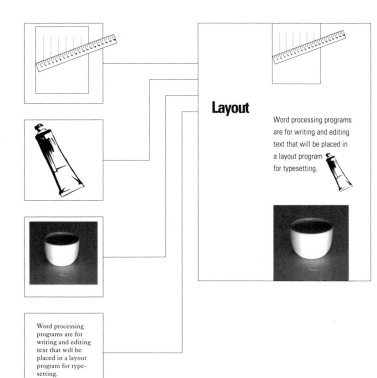

Drawing programs are used to create object-oriented illustrations and designs such as logos in PICT and EPS formats.

Basic paint programs are used for sketching and for modifying low-resolution scans.

Image processing software enables us to work with near-photographic quality images in formats such as PICT and TIFF.

Word processing software is used for writing and editing text.

Layout

Word processing programs are for writing and editing text that will be placed in a layout program for typesetting.

Layout programs allow us to combine and scale different kinds of files and formats. Most layout programs include basic drawing and text editing features.

Word processing programs are for writing and editing text that will be placed in a layout program for typesetting.

Because there are so many computer-related products available, there is a temptation to buy more than you need. Unless you have unlimited funds at your disposal, your initial investment should be modest—a computer system that is powerful enough to run the software you want to use; a laser printer; and basic graphic software. A layout program may be the only software you need at first. Once you have developed some proficiency, you will have a better idea of what your hardware and software needs are.

It is easy to get caught up in the excitement of the technology; many people find in retrospect that they bought much more than they needed. (Computer enthusiasts have much in common with camera buffs who spend so much time researching and buying the equipment that they never have time to learn to use it.)

Do not become overly concerned with speed—until you have become very proficient, you will be the slow part of the system, not the computer; most systems can be upgraded easily. Avoid duplicating functions, particularly if funds are limited; for example, if you buy a Macintosh SE with a built-in screen, use your remaining funds to buy a laser printer rather than a large screen. Do not try to anticipate your needs too far in advance; hardware is evolving at such a rapid rate that experts recommend that you update or replace your equipment every two years (and software evolves even more rapidly).

SERVICE BUREAUS

Service bureau is a catch-all phrase that can refer to any one of a number of services related to desktop technology. These include: businesses that allow you to rent time on computers, print on laser printers, and use peripherals such as scanners; businesses that offer desktop publishing services, including typesetting and layout from your instructions, and laser printing files from your disks; and businesses that provide only Linotronic output and prepress services. The range of services and levels of quality are often confusing. Explain your project needs carefully before ordering work from a service bureau to ensure that they offer the appropriate services and level of quality. If you are using a computer for comps and do not have a laser printer, for example, your needs will not be the same as a desktop publisher who considers laser printing as final art, nor will it be the same when you are generating camera-ready or prepress art. It is not uncommon to use one vendor for the comping phase of a project and another for the production phase.

BASICS

9-by-12-inch tracing pad

9-by-12-inch marker pad

Assorted black markers

Assorted colored markers

Mechanical pencil

Refill lead

Soft eraser

Pica-inch ruler

Parallel rule or t-square

30°/60° triangle

Art knife with #11 blades

Cutting mat

Lupe

Drawing board

Repositionable lamp

Portable lightbox

White tape

Magic Plus tape

Spray adhesive

Bestine

PMS swatchbook

OPTIONAL:

Rubber cement

Desk brush

Swabs and wipes

Steel straightedge

45° triangle

COMPUTER-RELATED:

Basic hardware

SKETCHING

9-by-12-inch vellum pad

9-by-12-inch ledger pad

Pencil sharpener

BUY AS NEEDED:

Colored markers

Colored pencils

Drawing templates

French curves

Flexible curve guide

Marker sprayer

OPTIONAL:

Assorted grid paper

Blending markers

Brush pens

Drafting pens

COMPUTER-RELATED:

Paint software

COMPING

Mounting board

Cover stock

Frisket material

Compass for cutting

Burnisher

Desk brush

Calculator

Color reference

Typography reference

BUY AS NEEDED:

Pantone papers and films

Other papers and films

Mounting board

Cover stock

Commercial stock

Transfer type

Word positioning refills

Double-sided tape

Black photographic tape

OPTIONAL:

Acrylic or goauche paint

Ruling pen

Compass with ruling pen

Paint brushes

Proportional scale

Color Tag system

Tape dispenser

Flat storage

COMPUTER-RELATED:

Drawing software

Layout software

Scanner

Laser printer

OUTSIDE SERVICES

Photocopying

Typesetting

Photostats

Custom transfers

Color photocopies

COMPUTER-RELATED:

Laser printing

Scanning

Linotronic output

Color printouts

3

3

Section 3 introduces a variety of information and procedures that can help streamline the visualization process.

When the designer is developing and visualizing an idea, he or she should not also be struggling with the mechanics of visualization. Visualization techniques must become second nature to the designer because they are so much an integral part of the design process. The better the designer's visualization skills, and the greater the designer's understanding of the methods for visualizing on paper or screen, the more time that can be spent on thinking about design. A designer who lacks specific visualization skills is often tempted to ignore an idea that he or she cannot comp or sketch. Drawing techniques, such as scaling and perspective, which may have been introduced to the reader in other contexts such as an art or geometry class, are reintroduced in the context of visualization. Basic color theory and how it applies to the materials and processes used in graphic design are also introduced in this section, as are basic techniques and procedures for cutting, masking, assembling, and finishing a sketch or comp.

PREPARATION AND SET-UP

One of the key things designers learn when they start meeting deadlines is the importance of organization and planning; in fact, *planning* is a synonym for *design*. It is not uncommon to spend at least as much time setting up to work on a design project as it takes do the work itself. Good preparation enables the designer to work quickly. Preparing a few underlays in advance, for example, allows the designer to focus on layout and the potential relationships between the elements in the layout. With positioning guides such as grids, the designer can avoid redrawing the same lines over and over and can avoid drawing guidelines directly on the comp. Many of the underlays used early in the process are often reused later.

Other techniques, such as masking and assembly, allow the designer to work quickly without sacrificing neatness. Some of these set-up techniques are borrowed from illustrators and industrial designers, who must be able to work quickly; some are borrowed from production artists, who must be able to work accurately.

TECHNIQUES AND TECHNOLOGY

Most of the procedures, techniques, and information presented in this section are useful no matter what kind of tools you work with or what kind of technology you use. Many of the techniques included in this section have been used for centuries, transcending boundaries of culture, discipline, and technology. Construction techniques that date from classic Greek geometry, for example, are as convenient to use on the computer screen as on paper. Underlays have been commonly used by artists, illustrators, industrial designers, and architects for decades to provide structure and reference points. The techniques we use for showing perspective were refined and popularized during the Renaissance, as was the use of isometric drawing to create the illusion of depth in patterns.

New technologies spawn new techniques. Photographic technology, developed more than a century ago, introduced whole new ways of working. Today, designers use photographs, send out for photostats, and make photocopies as part of the natural order of things—few can imagine a time when the only way to copy something or to make it a different size was to redraw it. Computers will have at least as much impact as photography on the techniques we use, but we will also continue to rely on some of the basic techniques from the past. On the computer, for example, the concept of tracing paper underlays has been translated into templates, layers, and reference guidelines.

Underlays are drawing or positioning guides that are placed under the sketch or comp for tracing and reference. Almost anything can be an underlay—text from a magazine, a rough sketch, a grid, or a logo. By using underlays, we can trace without drawing preliminary lines or guides directly on a sketch or comp. Because underlays are reusable, we do not need to draw the same information more than once. When underlays are drawn on tracing paper, several can be used at once. Layout elements that are drawn on separate underlays can be repositioned independently. As the underlays for a layout are rearranged, the designer gets a preview of each potential composition. The designer can rearrange the underlays to explore a wide range of layout options, recording the best compositions by tracing them as roughs. The roughs can then be evaluated and refined, using the same underlays again.

Because there are an infinite number of possible design solutions for any design problem, we must focus on a limited number of possibilities. Underlays, by nature, exclude options. When we use a specific grid as an underlay for a layout, for example, we are excluding other grids which would yield other layout results. For this reason, underlays should be used only after the preliminary thinking and sketching phase, so that the underlays created or selected relate to an overall design direction.

At the same time, underlays encourage the designer to explore a wider range of possible ways to combine a fixed set of elements. This makes underlays a particularly useful way to work when the time allocated for developing a design is extremely limited, or when the designer finds that he or she has run out of ideas or needs a wider variety of ideas. Variety can be ensured simply by changing the underlays being used—seeing a key element in a different size or using a different grid creates a whole new array of layout options. Rather than have too few ideas, or too many similar ones, the designer may find that he or she has the opposite problem—too many from which to choose.

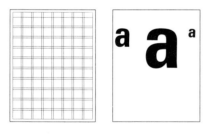

Only these two underlays were used to create this array of layout sketches. More variations were possible. Text was indicated by drawing a consistent number of lines per grid field.

—PAGE PROPORTIONS AND SCALE. Unless the paper you are working on is the same size as the sketch or comp you are developing, you will need an underlay that shows the edges of the layout. The page frame does not need to be actual size, but it should retain the correct proportion and should be lightly traced on each sketch (see *Construction Techniques* in this section).

—MINIMUM MARGINS are the narrowest margins possible within printing and binding requirements. They are not necessarily the actual margins that will be used in a layout. When minimum margins are included on the page frame, they act as a reminder of these requirements.

—GRIDS AND MARGINS. A *grid* for layout can be a simple pattern of lines that subdivide the page into a regular pattern of squares or rectangles, much like printed grid paper, or it can be a more complex *typographic grid* that divides the page into a regular pattern of *fields* separated by *intervals* of space. Unless the grid being used is part of a corporate identity system, it is independent of margins, that is, it can be positioned within the minimum margins in a number of ways. The position of the grid on the page frame determines the actual margins that will be used for the layout. Simply by moving the grid within the minimum margins, different layout effects are achieved.

—POSITIONING GUIDES are lines that are used for establishing locations for elements and for aligning elements within established locations. A grid can be thought of as a network of positioning guides, but positioning guides are not necessarily grids. Positioning guides may be as simple as a centering line or some key location points for specific elements.

—AN EXISTING LAYOUT can be used as an underlay, and key positioning guides can be drawn for matching the layout's structure. This is often useful if you are trying to create a companion piece. By tracing the guides directly from the layout rather than measuring and translating the measurements into a set of guides, the designer saves considerable time during the design process.

—TEXT UNDERLAYS lend a look of realism to your text indication that cannot be achieved by simply drawing a pattern of lines. It is important to use an underlay on which text has been set in the correct point size and with the correct leading. Although it is not critical that the underlay be the correct typeface if all of the other type specifications are satisfactory, using the correct typeface will provide you with a general idea of how many words will fit on the layouts you create and will give a general idea of color and texture. If you are not working at actual size, be sure to scale your text underlays accordingly.

—DISPLAY TYPE UNDERLAYS. Display type cannot just be indicated—it must be traced letter by letter, and spaces between letters must be optically even. Transfer lettering is an efficient way to create a display type underlay because the letters are already perfectly drawn—the designer is free to focus on kerning, word spacing, line breaks, and leading. Tracing type to use as an underlay is almost always more time consuming than using transfer letters and does not give us as accurate an underlay with which to work.

Transfer lettering may pose problems, however. It is not always available in the desired size and style, and we must take care that we do not sacrifice an essential design element to the availability of a supply. The typefaces we find as transfers are not always available to our typesetter, so we should cross reference what we choose as an underlay.

If you use a desktop computer or have typesetting equipment available, you can set display type in a range of point sizes, leadings, and line lengths very quickly. Typesetting can provide a wider selection of underlays from which to choose, and these underlays can often be created in a relatively short amount of time.

Whether you are tracing type, using transfers, or setting type on a desktop system, make sure that the type you use is available in the typesetting system that will be used for setting the camera-ready type.

Type specimens were used as underlays to create this group of type sketches. Even when a designer will be using a computer for tight comps, he or she may prefer to do preliminary sketches by hand. *(James Gidley)*

—SCALING. Photographically reducing or enlarging type after it has been set should be a last resort for two reasons: first, you will not know what size type you are indicating; second, type spaces do not scale at the same rate as the letterforms themselves. When type is reduced, spaces between letters get tighter; when type is enlarged, spaces get too wide. If you need to enlarge and reduce the display type underlays you create so that you have more options to work with, anticipate the optical changes in spacing caused by rescaling. Only consider rescaling as an option when you can have type set to any point size for the camera-ready art.

UNDERLAYS FOR SYMBOL DEVELOPMENT

When you sketch ideas for symbols, each sketch may be an underlay for the next. In this way, ideas are refined and developed in response to the feedback the designer gets from seeing the idea on paper. A symbol sketch can be the beginning of several design directions—each series of overlays branches in a new direction, and any one sketch may serve as the beginning of several new branches.

In addition to sketches, underlays for symbols may include standard grid paper for quick measurement and alignment and reference in the form of geometric shapes, letterforms, photographs, or spot illustrations. Virtually anything can act as a guide for the development of a form.

Combinations of underlays inspire new ideas. Each sketch can become an underlay, or part of an underlay, for the next. The same underlay traced with different tools or viewed in a different way may inspire even more design ideas.

USING UNDERLAYS

Using multiple underlays may be distracting and discouraging at first because they are difficult to handle. For recording ideas, underlays need only be loosely aligned. For more refined sketches and for comps, however, underlays must be carefully aligned and fixed in position so that they retain their positions and relationships as you work with them. Make sure the underlays are aligned squarely by positioning them with your parallel rule or t-square. Underlays such as page frames, grids, and type can be taped together temporarily with Magic Plus tape. This "sandwich" can then be taped either to your drawing pad, your lightbox, or even the back of the paper on which you are drawing. Take care to place the tape outside the work area whenever possible so that it does not interfere with your drawing. When you find a combination of underlays that you will be reusing, or that you will be using for a comp, you may find it helpful to photocopy it or retrace it onto one layer.

—UNDERLAYS WITH OPAQUE PAPERS. Working on the lightbox with underlays makes using opaque papers as easy to use as tracing paper, and you can avoid drawing guides directly on the paper itself. If the paper is particularly opaque, you may need to redraw the underlays with black marker or ink—if you are tracing a sandwich of underlays, this is a perfect opportunity to trace them onto a single sheet. You may wish to tape the underlays into position face down on the back of the comping paper rather than try to align one with the other on the lightbox.

Construction techniques rely on a few simple principles of geometry and do not use numbers or arithmetic, only drawing. Constructions allow us to work quickly; by learning to work quickly, we have more time for design because we spend less time on such mechanical tasks as measuring.

DIAGONALS

A *diagonal* is a line drawn between opposite corners of a rectangle. Diagonals can be used for comparing proportions, for scaling, and for subdividing rectangles. Diagonals drawn across a rectangle *intersect* (meet) at its center, so drawing two diagonals is a fast and easy way to find the center of a rectangle, such as a page. If vertical and horizontal lines are drawn through the point where the diagonals intersect, each edge of the rectangle is divided in half, and the area is divided into quarters. One of these quarters is the equivalent of a 50 percent reduction. Subdividing with diagonals works in increments of four (2^2)—as you can see in the diagram below, each rectangle is subdivided into four smaller ones.

Notice that the diagonals in each progressively smaller rectangle are parallel. When the diagonals of two rectangles are parallel, we know that they have the same proportions. This means that to scale a rectangle up or down (larger or smaller) along its diagonal, we have copied the proportions of the rectangle exactly. To quickly draw a small rectangle that represents an 8½-by-11-inch sheet of paper, for example, we can simply draw a diagonal on a sheet of 8½-by-11-inch paper and then draw a rectangle to any size so long as its corners align with that diagonal.

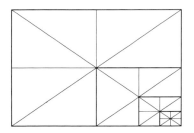

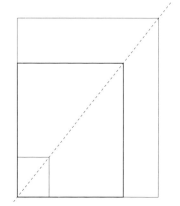

SUBDIVIDING SPACE IN ANY INCREMENTS

If we wish to subdivide a length into an uneven number of increments, we can use another technique that also lets us avoid arithmetic and calculation. This technique requires that you have a scale longer than the length of the line being subdivided. It does not matter what scale is used—inches, millimeters, picas—because the number relationships stay the same. Place the zero-mark of the scale at one edge of the length and rotate it until the number of divisions you want aligns at the opposite edge, then make a mark on the paper at each whole number along the scale. If, for example, you wish to divide an 11-inch-wide space into 17 sections, simply place your scale at a diagonal so that the zero-mark is at one edge and the 17-mark at the other, then mark the paper at every whole mark along the way. To divide this 11-inch length into 34 sections, you could make a small mark on the paper at every half mark as well as every whole mark (2 x 17= 34). Done carefully, this method can be remarkably accurate and is faster and easier than dividing and plotting with math.

USING SCALE INCREMENTS

A simple but time-saving technique is to tape a scale in place rather than go through the several steps it takes to hold a scale in position, draw tick marks, remove it, and then align a straightedge with each tick mark drawn. By taping a scale into position, no preliminary marks need to be drawn. The Precision Rules described in section 2, or any similar paper-thin scales, are ideal for this technique. Layout and drawing software have the computer equivalent of this in the form of rulers that appear along the top and side of the screen, to which you can align elements as you work. Just as you can reposition the scale taped down so that the zero mark is at a handy place, you can reposition the zero-mark on the rulers in most software.

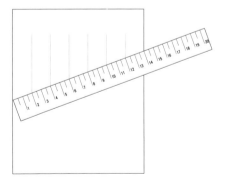

SCALING WITH A GRID

One of the ways many of us learned to scale something up was by drawing a grid of squares on the original image, then drawing a grid with larger squares on our paper. What appeared in each of the small squares was what we drew in each of the larger corresponding squares. If you have a grid printed on clear acetate, and a grid of larger squares as an underlay, this is still a relatively fast and accurate way to sketch something to a different scale, and it has the advantage of helping you draw what you see—by looking at an object square by square, you are more apt to draw what is before your eyes and less likely to try to draw from memory.

USING A CALCULATOR FOR PROPORTIONING

If you are familiar with a calculator and basic math, you will find that it is more accurate to use a calculator than a proportion wheel for scaling something up and down. There are several methods for doing this. Remember that if your calculator doesn't have a percentage feature you will need to add a decimal point. If you order a photostat shot at 100 percent, you will get something that is the same size as the original (100% = 1). If you order a photostat shot at 500 percent, it will be five times larger than the original (500% = 5). To scale, divide a new dimension by an old one. To find out the percentage needed to make a 4-inch line into a 6-inch line, for example, divide 6 by 4—the result is 1.5, or 150 percent. To make a 7-inch line into a 2-inch line, divide 2 by 7—the result is .2857, which is midway between 28 and 29 percent.

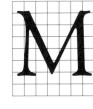

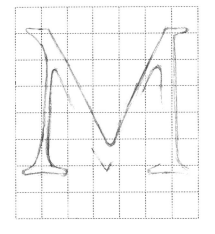

A ratio can be used to find an unknown dimension. If we wanted to enlarge a 4-by-5-inch rectangle, and we knew that we wanted the 4-inch length to be 6 inches, our ratio would read 4:5 = 6:?, or, *four is to five as six is to what?* Multiply inside numbers together and outside numbers together. Because there is an unknown number (the number we want to find so we know the size of the new rectangle), multiply the known numbers—5 and 6. Divide the result, 30, by the remaining known number, 4, to find the unknown number—30 ÷ 4 = 7.5. Put the unknown number into the original ratio—4:5 = 6:7.5. This means that a 4-by-5-inch rectangle has the same proportion as a 6-by-7.5-inch rectangle.

COPYING ANGLES

To enlarge a complex shape such as a letter, draw a box around the original shape, scale the box to the desired size by using its diagonal, then draw radiating lines through the key points in the original drawing to the edges of the larger box. These radiating lines meet the edges of the larger box where the new shape will be. Trace the angles, then connect lines.

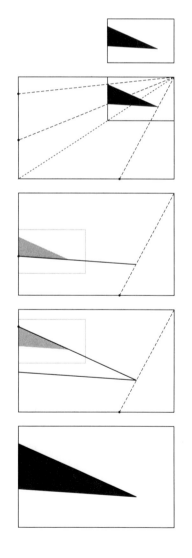

ISOMETRIC DRAWING

An *isometric* drawing, generally speaking, is one in which angles showing depth are fixed, that is, they do not converge at a distance as optical perspective lines do (see *Perspective* in this section). Isometric drawing is common in drafting, but it is less common when a three-dimensional object is being drawn to look real. Isometric drawing allows you to draw a three-dimensional shape without using true (optical) perspective. In an isometric drawing, all of the edges that are not vertical or horizontal are at a fixed angle, such as 30°. Because the angles are consistent, isometric shapes such as the cubes shown below can be assembled into interesting tiling patterns that give the illusion of depth. Such patterns were used during the Renaissance in such things as the flooring tiles in cathedrals to create the illusion of depth. Postmodern furniture and architecture are often presented in isometric format because of its highly decorative quality. To give three-dimensional objects a realistic look, however, we must use optical perspective.

In the three-dimensional world, objects look smaller when they are far away from us and larger when they are near. *Perspective* enables us to determine how to draw the lines on a two-dimensional surface to indicate the correct changes in size and distance. Although perspective is a complex subject and requires study, the principles shown here will provide the graphic designer with enough information to use perspective in sketches and photo indications.

Perspective drawing begins with a construction diagram in which one or more vanishing points are established along a horizon line. The horizon line represents eye level; we are looking up at objects drawn above the horizon line and down at objects drawn below it. Objects get progressively smaller as they move away from us and parallel lines get closer together.

Once a grid has been drawn in perspective, it can be used for plotting shapes just as it can when flat.

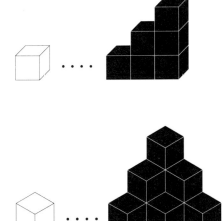

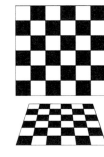

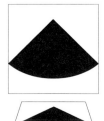

ONE-POINT PERSPECTIVE

One-point perspective is used to draw an object that has a side you are viewing straight on, or an edge that is horizontal (parallel to the horizon line). In one-point perspective, vertical lines stay vertical and horizontal lines stay horizontal. The only lines that are drawn to the vanishing point are those that represent edges moving away from us in space.

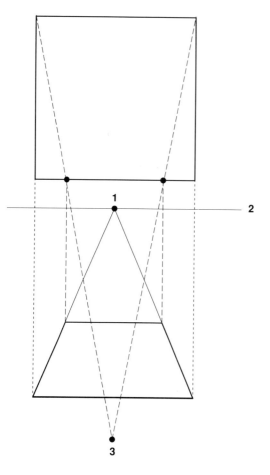

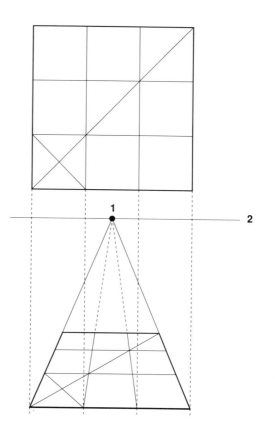

To draw a square in one-point perspective, draw the basic elements of a perspective diagram: the vanishing point (1), the horizon line (2), and the observation point (3). Draw a square above the horizon line, centering it on the vanishing point. Extend its vertical sides down below the horizon line, then draw a horizontal line between them. This becomes the edge of the square nearest the viewer.

Draw lines that recede from the ends of this line to the vanishing point. This shows how the width of the square diminishes as it recedes. To find the back edge of the square, connect the top corners of the original square to the observation point. Where these lines intersect the bottom of the original square, draw vertical lines down to the receding lines. A horizontal line at this intersection is the back edge of the square.

To make the square into a grid, extend the vertical subdivisions from the bottom edge of the original square to the front edge of the perspective square. Where the diagonal crosses a subdivision line, draw a horizontal line. Each of the squares created can be further subdivided with diagonals.

TWO-POINT PERSPECTIVE

Two-point perspective is used when the edges of an object are not parallel to the horizon line. (With this stipulation in mind, we can see that one- and two-point perspective might be combined in a single drawing if we are viewing a number of objects that have different orientations.)

In this simplified two-point perspective diagram, a square is projected to become the base of a cube. The observation point has been eliminated.
The height of the cube is determined by using a side of the flat square (*bc*) as a radius to draw an arc that intersects the horizontal line running through point *b*.

A line is projected from this intersection to a horizontal line drawn through point B, and another arc is drawn up to mark the height of the vertical line drawn from B. Just as in other perspective diagrams, corners are determined by intersecting lines drawn to vanishing points.

In this diagram a square grid is projected into two-point perspective. The flat grid is placed above the horizon line at a 45° angle; a line is drawn parallel to the horizon line to mark the front edge of the square (4). The corners of the square are projected to a viewing point, just as in the one-point perspective drawings.

Where these projection lines intersect line 4, vertical lines are drawn. Corners A and C are determined where these vertical lines intersect the lines drawn from corner B to the vanishing points.

The objective of isometric and perspective drawing is to represent depth (three-dimensional space) on a two-dimensional surface, such as a sheet of paper. We can enhance the illusion of depth we create in a number of ways: overlapping shapes to imply front and back; making lines and elements bolder and crisper where they are nearer to us; by adding shadow; and by showing the *modeling* (light and shading on a form). Of these, overlapping shapes is the most powerful because it establishes a definite front-and-back relationship. We see more surface details on nearby objects than on those that are far away. Nearby objects have more contrast than far-away objects. People often comment that far-away objects seem closer on a clear day.

When detail is included on far-away objects, the illusion of depth tends to be diminished. Many computer-generated illustrations have a flat look because detail and contrast do not diminish on objects that are supposed to be far away. Not only do our eyes see less contrast and detail in far-away objects, but colors are softened and edges are not as crisp. Product illustrators find that a drawing has more depth when a little extra contrast and clarity is added to the parts nearest the viewer, and that edges farther away are softer and have less contrast. Although this does not necessarily lend realism to a small object such as a toaster, it enhances the feeling of three dimensions.

Contrast and size establish a visual hierarchy—the objects we notice first are those that have the most contrast and are the largest. Even forms we know are flat can be used to create a composition that has depth if we follow these same rules.

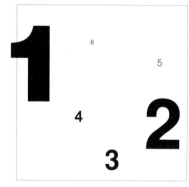
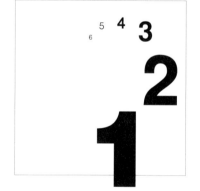

Even when we know we are seeing elements on a flat surface, we may see them as moving away from us in three-dimensional space. Only one or two depth-illusion principles need to be used to create this effect.

LIGHT AND SHADOW

We are able to see objects because they reflect light. The nature of light is an integral part of the image we see; a drawing of an image implies some kind of lighting. When the light is *diffuse*—that is, it does not seem to be coming from any specific direction—we see only soft shadow. When light is coming from a specific source, objects will have a shaded side and will cast a distinct shadow. When we draw, such as for a photo indication, it is the pattern of light and shadow that we show on the paper. Objects often cast shadows on one another; when one object casts a shadow on the other, their relationship in space is clearly established. Modeling indicates how a surface is shaped; a circle can become a sphere, for example, only when the light and shadow are indicated on the surface of the circle.

The contrast between light and shadow helps us establish the feeling of depth. We tend to think of light as coming from above; a circle that is modeled with its lightest area at the top is generally seen as a bump; when the lightest area is at the bottom it is seen as a depression.

Value is the lightness or darkness of an object in relation to its surroundings. The value of the object determines the value of the shadow; shadows, then, are not all the same value. The shadow side of a white box, for example, is of a lighter value than the shadow side of a dark one, and the shadow cast on a wooden table will be of a darker value than the shadow cast on a white one.

All four of these images of a white cup on a white table were created with the same camera angle and the same light. The only difference between them is the position of the light.

When you are cutting a comp, you are simulating the exact cuts made by commercial, large-scale paper cutters or dies, and your cuts should reflect this precision. To cut accurately and cleanly, you must use a sharp blade, an even pressure, and a low blade angle. An X-acto knife with a #11 blade or its equivalent has become a standard tool for graphics because the blade has a sharp enough angle to allow you to cut curved lines. Do not hold the knife perpendicular to the paper when you cut; keep it at an angle so that you are cutting with about the bottom third of the blade edge. When cutting a straight line, place the straightedge on the part of the paper you will be using, not the part you are cutting off. In this way, if your blade strays from the straightedge, it will not ruin your work. Hold the straightedge firmly in place. Cut on a clean, clear surface; a cutting mat is recommended. Turn your work so that you have a good cutting angle; most people cut better lines when they pull the blade toward them than when they cut from left to right.

—CUTTING CORNERS. When you are cutting shapes with corners, begin and end your cuts beyond the corners. Because the blade edge is not perpendicular to the surface of the paper, you cannot always see where your blade actually begins and ends cutting; often the initial pressure of cutting deflects the blade and the first part of the cut is not straight.

—CUTTING A COMPLEX SHAPE. If you are cutting paper into a complex shape such as a letterform, draw the shape on tracing paper, spray-mount it face down on the back of the paper, and cut from the back. By sticking the cutting guide to the paper you are cutting, the guide cannot shift out of place during cutting and handling. Although most of the time you will be cutting a shape to stick onto a background, if the shape has intricate details or tiny pieces, you may want to cut holes in the background paper instead.

—CUTTING A FRISKET. Make sure the frisket you are using has a low tack adhesive so that it will not damage the paper on which you are working. If you are using frisket on a relatively translucent paper, use an underlay as a positioning and cutting guide and work on a lightbox. If you are working on opaque paper or do not have a lightbox, you can trace directly on the matte frisket, then position the frisket on the comp. Always use a sharp blade so that you can use a minimum of pressure and cut only through the frisket, not through the comping paper as well. The amount of pressure you need will be influenced by the backing surface you cut on, so it is wise to practice a few cuts before you begin.

—CUTTING A DIE LINE. When you make a package mock-up or a presentation folder you will need to cut it to shape. If both sides of the paper are to show in your comp, you will not want to spray-mount your cutting guide to your paper or draw on your paper. Instead, cut a pattern out of medium-weight scrap paper, such as a paper bag or tag board, and lay it on top of the paper you are going to cut. If you are making a folder or box that matches an existing die, use a folder or box made from that die as your pattern (you will need to pull any glued tabs apart to get the piece to lay flat). If you will be working on a lightbox, mark the corners with a sharp blade or pin; light coming through the holes will be easy to see. Otherwise, mark the corners with a fine-tipped pen or pencil. Remove the pattern and cut between the holes or marks with a straightedge.

—CUTTING AN EMBOSSING DIE. Although intricate, multiple-level embossing dies cannot be easily simulated with paper, most embossing dies are relatively easy to create. Cast-coated paper, available at many art stores, is an appropriate thickness and cuts more easily than two-ply bristol board, which is about the same weight. Acetate can also be used. The shape of the area to be embossed (raised) should be traced or drawn, then spray-mounted to the stock you are using as your die. Cut along the shape so that you are left with a hole in the shape you want to emboss. If the shape has details within it that do not emboss, you will need to spray-mount the die face down on another piece of stock, then spray-mount the detail shapes in place as well. Let the adhesive set up before you use the die (see *Embossing* in section 4).

—CUTTING A DEBOSSING DIE. A debossing die is cut from the same kind of stock as an embossing die, but instead of cutting a hole, cut the shape and spray-mount it face down to another surface.

—CUTTING ARCS AND CIRCLES. To cut an *arc* (a segment of a circle) or a circle, you need a compass that will hold a knife with a #11 blade or its equivalent. The compass must hold the knife firmly. If you prefer, use a compass that holds a cutting blade in place of a pencil lead (see *Comping Materials and Tools* in section 2). Unless the inside of the circle is to drop away, protect the area on which the point rests by making a cushion of Magic Plus tape or by cutting a small piece of eraser that will not slide out of position from the pressure applied during the cutting of the circle. If the point will penetrate the paper you are cutting, cut on a piece of cardboard or chipboard rather than on a cutting mat so that the compass needle will hold firmly.

The cutting edge of the blade should face the direction in which you will cut. Keep the compass angle low so that you are using the cutting edge of the blade rather than just the tip, and make multiple passes with light pressure until the blade has cut through. If too much pressure is applied, the blade will be deflected slightly and will not cut an even path. You may find it easier to rotate the paper than to move the blade. Circle cutting requires some practice, but the results are impressive. To measure the size of the circle you are cutting, place the centerpoint of the compass on the zero-mark on a scale and then adjust the compass so that the cutting blade is on the mark that measures the *radius* of the circle (half the overall width, or diameter). To cut a 3-inch circle, for example, put the center point on the zero-mark and the cutting tip on the 1-½-inch-mark (half the overall width).

Masking is the blocking off of areas to protect them.
A mask can be as simple as a sheet of tracing paper
taped in place with Magic Plus tape or as complex as a
symbol cut from a frisket. Magic Plus tape is particularly useful wherever you are drawing multiple lines
to an edge, such as the justified edge of text indication.
When you mask for spraying, either isolate the entire
surface with frisket, or cut a hole in a piece of tracing
paper that is a little larger than the area to be sprayed,
and tape the edges of the hole with Magic Plus tape.
When spraying an area, always keep in mind that
overspray covers a larger area than usually anticipated.
If equipment or walls are nearby, you will want to cover
these, as well as your work surface.

Whether you are creating sketches or comps, making
separate parts and then assembling them will give
you more options and save you the problem of redoing
an entire piece when only one element needs to be
redone. The basic rule for deciding which elements
can be created as separate pieces is whether or not it
creates a visible edge. A photo indication, for example,
usually has a visible edge, that is, you would see
the edge of the photo indication whether it was created
directly on the layout or trimmed and mounted in
place. A block of text, however, should not have a
visible edge around it. A text area created separately
would show an edge that would not be visible if the
text was created in place, so it must be created directly
on the comp. As a guideline, consider that where a
color break (edge) occurs, a cut line could exist without
being visible as a cut.

—ASSEMBLY SEQUENCE. Create all of the elements that must go directly on the sketch or comp and all of the elements that will be created separately and added to it. Working with your t-square or parallel rule, and using an underlay as a guide, position the elements to confirm position and size before spray-mounting them. Do subassemblies first; for example, if a diagram has a colored border, trim the diagram, spray-mount it onto a larger sheet of colored paper, trim the colored paper to the width of the border, then spray-mount it to the layout.

—TRIMMING. Elements that bleed should be left oversized on the bleed edges. Final edges should not be trimmed until all of the elements are in place. On folded pieces, do the final trim after it is folded and bound, smoothing from the binding out. Leave the front cover slightly oversized (about ⅟16 inch) along the right edge so that the piece opens easily. If the cover has some curvature, the front will still cover the inside and back of the piece.

—LAMINATING is the sandwiching together of two or more sheets of paper or other material, allowing it to be used as a single sheet. To indicate a cover that is printed on both sides, one side of which is coated, a coated stock and an uncoated stock might be laminated together. The total weight (thickness) of the lamination should be considered carefully. If the coated and uncoated papers are spray-mounted on either side of a sheet of cover stock, for example, the result will be too thick; if they are laminated only to each other, the result may be too thin. Laminated paper does not always fold well; often, the paper on the inside of the cover will buckle because it is being compressed into less space while the outside of the cover is being stretched. If the laminated cover has pages saddle-stitched inside it, cut a separate inside sheet for the front and the back and laminate them so that there is a slight gap at the score.

—SCORING AND FOLDING. *Scoring* is the compressing of the paper fibers to guide a fold. As a rule, folding should never be done without scoring first. Scoring should be done along a straightedge or guide in the desired shape; scoring can be done with a common metal paper clip or with a narrow edge of a burnisher.

Tracing paper was used as a simple mask for applying color with a marker sprayer.

A common metal paper clip makes an excellent scoring tool.

—SADDLE-STITCHING. Once pages have been scored, they can be aligned, clipped, or taped together at the top and bottom and saddle-stitched using a common desk stapler that opens flat. To saddle-stitch with a desk stapler, you must press the staples through the scored paper without bending the ends of the staples. To do this, either staple onto a sheet of corrugated cardboard, from which the stapled pages are easily lifted, or hang the scored line just beyond the edge of a table edge or thick pad so that the staple penetrates only the pages to be bound. Once the pages are saddle-stitched, bend the ends of the staples over by hand.

—FIXING MISTAKES. Avoid *any* patching or retouching to correct mistakes. Familiar techniques, such as putting white paint or paper on a smudge, will fool a camera but will not fool the eye. If a mistake is relatively minor, repairing it may draw more attention to it. If a mistake is not so minor that it cannot be left as is, redo the piece. Repaired comps and sketches distract from their main business of communicating a design idea and may have negative connotations as well.

A color has three basic characteristics: *saturation* (intensity), *value* (light-dark), and *hue* (what we usually call color; e.g., red, green). Any relationship between colors is based on all three of these characteristics. Because color is *relative*, the combination of colors we see influences how we see any one color; for example, we see a color as *warm* (reddish) or *cool* (bluish), or dark or light, only in relation to the colors around it. We may consider a gray dot on a white square as being dark, but the same gray dot on a black square will appear light. Contrast is an important part of color relationships. Colors can contrast with one another by a single characteristic (e.g., red and green could contrast in hue but not in value or saturation) or a combination of characteristics (e.g., yellow and violet may contrast in value and saturation as well as hue).

A desk stapler can be used for saddle-stitching if the scored line overhangs the edge of a backing so that the staples penetrate only the comp itself. The staples can then be turned down be hand.

THE COLOR WHEEL

Traditional color theory is best explained with the *color wheel*, the structured arrangement and relationship of hues. *Primary* hues (generally referred to as *primary colors*, or *primaries*) are the basic colors needed to mix all others; primary colors in the color wheel are red, yellow, and blue. A *secondary* color is produced when two adjacent primary colors on the color wheel are mixed. Secondary colors are orange (red plus yellow), green (yellow plus blue), and violet (blue plus red). A basic color wheel is made up of primary and secondary colors, and a primary color is always opposite a secondary color. Any two colors opposite one another on the color wheel are called *complements*, or *complementary* colors. Complementary colors contain all three primaries. Mixing any two adjacent primary and secondary colors together produce a *tertiary* color, such as red-orange (orange plus red). Although all colors can be mixed from primaries in theory, this proves to be difficult in practice, because in most mediums, such as paints, pure primaries do not exist. A traditional color palette, then, consists of both primaries and secondaries plus black and white. Black and white are used to change value but not hue.

PROCESS COLORS

Process colors, on which four-color process printing is based, use magenta, yellow, and cyan (a specific shade of blue) as primaries. Black is added as the fourth process color; in process printing, white comes from the amount of paper showing through the tint screens. Process colors are printed directly on the paper in dots of different sizes, and the viewer's eye, seeing these colors simultaneously, mixes the color automatically (see *Color Printing* in section 1). You can see how process colors mix together by looking at any of the color images in this book through a lupe.

Process colors are an alternate set of primaries, and are used in the same way.

RED

VIOLET

ORANGE

BLUE

YELLOW

GREEN

A basic color wheel shows the relationship between primary and secondary colors.

When we select color, we must rely on how colors look rather than on what they are called. A green marker, for example, may have very little in common with the green of a leaf or a specific ink color. We can seldom rely on the medium we use to produce the color we want as is, that is, straight out of the tube, marker, or pencil. To get the specific color we want—one that has the correct hue, value, and intensity—we must usually mix it from two or more other colors. Mixing color is more like cooking and less like chemistry in that we cannot rely completely on formulas or mechanically measured proportions. Just as the cook must adjust the proportions of ingredients to get the overall taste correct, the color mixer should be prepared to adjust proportions and percentages to get just the right color. Formulas and percentages, like recipes, are only points of departure, partly because ingredients (e.g., basic paint colors and differences in paper whiteness) are not consistent.

In addition, each color medium influences the color we see—paint, printing ink, and color on the computer screen do not look alike—and this compounds the problem of matching color when we create a comp. Although we cannot always show exact colors, we can strive to establish the relationship between colors. Because our perception of color is relative, establishing the relationship between colors is as important as the color itself. (It is this failure to establish such a relationship, as much as the shift in color, that makes color photocopies and some color stats so unsatisfactory.) —EFFECTS OF LIGHTING. Light has a significant effect on the color you see. A single color viewed under fluorescent light, incandescent light, and sunlight may be seen as three different colors. It is ideal to have all three types of lighting available and to see the colors you choose or mix under all three lighting conditions. When mixing and matching color, also consider the lighting conditions under which the comp will be viewed; to make final color decisions, consider the kind of light in which the final printed piece will be seen.

All of these swatches would probably be called "orange" if viewed separately.

PROCESS TINTS AS MIXING GUIDES

When the printed piece you are working on will be printed only in process colors, you may want a process tint chart or book that shows process tint combinations. To match process tints, begin with a palette of paint colors that are as close as possible to process colors. (Because it is difficult to find accurate process-color paints, you will probably need to compensate with additional colors.) If you are using paints that approximate process colors, begin with the proportions indicated by the tint screens in your reference chart or book, then adjust proportions until the color matches visually. Always rely on visual feedback rather than mechanical accuracy; how a color looks is more important than how carefully we have measured.

PANTONE FORMULAS AS MIXING GUIDES

Pantone colors are mixed from a set of basic colors that look somewhat like the colors in a color wheel or a rainbow: yellow, warm red, rubine red, rhodamine red, purple, reflex blue, process blue, and green. These, plus black and white, make up all the Pantone Matching System (PMS) colors except the metallics. Each of the hundreds of colors in the Pantone system are shown with their mixing formulas in the *Color Formula Guide* swatchbook.

By finding paints that approximate Pantone's basic colors, we can use the formulas in the swatchbook as guides for mixing colors. When buying paints, hue is the most important characteristic to match because value can be lightened with white. So while it is difficult to find a paint color that matches rhodamine red, a magenta or red-violet paint may match in hue and will also match in value if mixed with white.

All four of these colors were mixed with process color markers. Colors mixed this way have a different character and quality than premixed colors. Color mixing significantly expands the range of colors on your palette.

MIXING MARKER COLORS

On most marker papers it is possible to put down a layer of marker color and then modify it by adding another. Some markers work better for this than others, and some marker papers accept layers of color better than others, so experiment. Increasing the range of values you have increases the possible colors you can mix, but you will need a wide range of hues and values to mix the colors you want. Begin by using medium to light values—each layer of color added will tend to darken the overall value. Whether you are using a marker sprayer or applying the marker directly on the paper, let the color dry between applications. If the color you create is too bright, applying a very light gray over the whole area will tone it down. A color's comple-ment often has a similar effect; for example, a green that is too bright can be dulled with a light pink (pale red), while a pale orange will quiet an overly bright blue. Mixing hues in this way tends to make marker colors more complex and adds richness.

COMBINING MARKER AND PENCIL

Using marker as a base and modifying color and value with colored pencils increases your palette and gives you more control over subtle color changes and modeling. This technique is especially useful in photo indications. Marker provides saturated color; pencil controls hue and value. Begin by laying down an even color of marker in each area of your sketch in a hue and value nearest the final color you wish to match. Once the marker is dry, color over it with colored pencils to modify its hue. Colored pencil over marker is an easy way to indicate soft shadow on light- and medium-value objects as well.

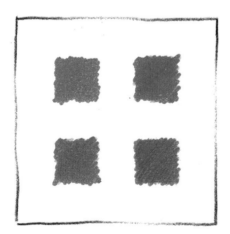

All four of these swatches started with the same blue marker (upper left). The upper right swatch was dulled with gray, the bottom left swatch was dulled with light orange, and blue pencil was used to tone the bottom right swatch.

If you don't have a lot of experience mixing and working with paint, you will need to set aside some time to practice so that you can learn how much paint to use, how much water to use, how to get an evenly mixed solution, and how to apply the paint to the comp. Because all paints vary in thickness—even the same brands of paint out of the same-sized tubes—there are no easy mixing formulas. Always take the time to mix paint thoroughly. Begin by putting some dabs of the paint colors you will be mixing on a flat, nonporous surface such as a white plastic palette or ceramic dish. (In general, plan to use at least twice as much white paint as any other color.) Transfer an appropriate amount of each color to a shallow container with a stick or brush. Add a small amount of water and begin mixing thoroughly, but not too vigorously, with a soft brush, adding water as needed. Mix until all of the colors have combined and the paint is the consistency of heavy cream (not skim milk, not yogurt). To test the color, brush a thin spot of paint onto the edge of a piece of paper that matches the paper you will be using. If you are trying to match a color swatch, keep in mind that the whiteness of the paper on which the swatch is printed will affect the color you see.

—COLOR SHIFTS DURING DRYING. If you are using acrylics, the paint will dry darker; if you are using gouache, the paint will dry lighter. Whenever possible, let the sample spot of color dry to be sure of a match. If you use acrylics, the paint you mix will harden into a plastic that will not rewet and cannot be reused, so only mix as much as you need or store mixed paint in an airtight container. (Storing it in a refrigerator will lengthen the amount of time it can be used.) Do not plan to cover large surfaces with paint—most comping papers do not accept wet media without warping and stretching. You can paint small pieces of paper and acetate to use as accent color (see *Accent color* in section 4).

—USING A RULING PEN. A *ruling pen* has two pointed blades between which is loaded a liquid medium, such as ink or paint. They were originally used for mechanical drawings instead of a brush because they make a line of a consistent width, and although ruling pens traditionally were used with ink, they are significantly easier to use with paint. With a ruling pen, it is possible to draw along a straightedge as well as freehand. The paint you put into the ruling pen must be the consistency of heavy cream to flow evenly but not too fast. It must be thick enough to remain opaque on the paper. Paint is put between the blades with a brush or eyedropper, not dipped like a drawing pen. Any paint that gets on the outside of the blades when you are loading the ruling pen should be wiped off before you draw. A screw controls the distance between the blades, and this distance determines the width of the line you will draw. If you want to draw a wide line, it is often better to draw two thinner lines marking the edges and then fill between them rather than set the blades of the pen far apart. A paint line is as deep as it is wide, so a wide line uses considerably more paint and takes a long time to dry.

—PAINTING ON PHOTOCOPIES. In developing forms for symbols and logotypes, it is sometimes more expedient to use a photocopier in the process of modifying a form than to continue to trace each form. Black paint allows you to add to a form; white paint allows you to subtract from a form. Black paint is a better choice than marker, which is likely to bleed through the white paint. In the examples below, a letterform has been photocopied and modified with white paint. The paint has been applied with a ruling pen and with a brush.

—PAINTING ON TREATED ACETATE. If you paint from the back so the painted area is viewed through the acetate, painted acetate provides a smooth, glossy finish that simulates gloss varnish or UV coating. Paint a small area, let it dry, then cut it to shape and spray-mount it with the painted surface down, or use acetate with an underlay to paint rules and shapes (put the underlay face down with the acetate face down on top of it, so that the paint is on the back rather than the front of the acetate when you are finished). Acetate curls slightly; work with it so that corners curl down when viewed from the front. Paint lines spread more on acetate than on paper surfaces and will tend to be wider than anticipated.

By painting directly on a photocopy of a shape, we can create a number of variations quickly; each variation can be photocopied and used as a point of departure for creating additional variations.

Although the quality of most comping and sketching materials is high, do not expect perfect consistency; too many factors are at work. The age of the product, how and where it was stored, and inconsistencies in the raw materials supplied to the manufacturer will cause a product to act and react differently. Slight differences from batch to batch may only show up in specific combinations of products or when you are using a specific technique. If you are drawing roughs, for example, a difference in black from marker to marker may seem insignificant, but the difference will become important in a tight sketch because it will imply that more than one color of black will be printed. The more accurate your visualization technique, the more critical slight differences become.

One of the most important habits to develop, whether you are working on sketches or comps, is that of testing materials and practicing techniques before you work directly on your piece. Although it is useful to test a wide range of products for a general comparison, anticipate testing the products again each time you work. Testing can be as simple as making a marker line on your test paper or checking to see how a particular shade of pencil will look over a marker background. Testing will save hours of redoing comps or sketches because the materials you used or the techniques you tried didn't work as anticipated.

Product labels do not guarantee consistency and predictability; for example, two nib sizes of the same marker brand may have completely different ink formulas, and two brands of rag marker paper are likely to have different surfaces, opacities, rag content, and whiteness.

—ADHESIVES. Pressure-sensitive adhesives change with time and storage conditions, and a paper, film, or frisket that seems to have an agreeably low-tack adhesive one day may grip like packing tape the next time you purchase it. An adhesive backing on a film or frisket that has too strong an adhesive will often tear the surface of the paper. If you have precut a shape and position it exactly right the first time, this is no problem. However, if you cut a shape in place and remove the excess film or frisket, or if you need to move or remove an element, surface tearing becomes a serious problem. Part of the problem is because of the nature of comping paper itself, in that both printed colors and surface coatings are superficial—beneath them is plain white paper. Attempts to patch a surface tear generally end up looking worse than the tear itself and will draw attention to the imperfection rather than hide it.

—MARKERS. Marker ink formulas vary, even within a brand. The intensity of the same color in the same brand can vary from marker to marker. In a set or series of markers, such as values of gray, value changes can be uneven and hue can vary considerably. A dark gray marker in a series, for example, may look blue and a lighter marker in the same series may be pinkish. Although such a color shift can be useful for drawing shadows in an illustration, it is unwanted in a sketch of a black-and-white printed piece or photograph indication.

—PAPER. Whatever paper you are working on or with, make sure that you have an extra piece of it available to test markers, paint, and adhesives before using them and to practice techniques such as painting, scoring, and cutting. The series below shows four papers and how they respond to the same series of markers and pencils. Each material and tool has its own characteristics; each has its advantages in specific situations.

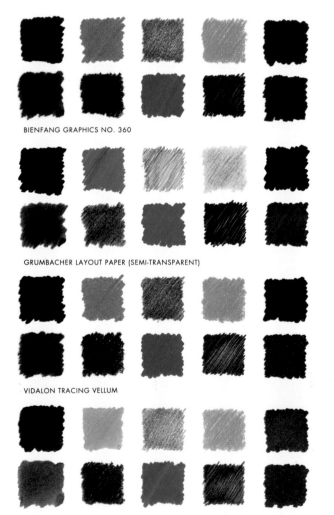

BIENFANG GRAPHICS NO. 360

GRUMBACHER LAYOUT PAPER (SEMI-TRANSPARENT)

VIDALON TRACING VELLUM

ARTTEC NO. 38 TRACING PAD

The same series of markers and pencils were used on different papers to compare color saturation, surface texture, and bleed.

When you look at the computer screen you are seeing *additive* rather than *subtractive* color, that is, colored light is transmitted directly to your eye rather than reflected off a surface. The value range you work with on the screen may be considerably different than what you work with on paper. This is because transmitted light can be much lighter and brighter than the white reflected off even the whitest paper. Some monitors are adjusted to compensate for this difference.

SCREEN COLOR BASICS

On most color computer systems you can specify color in a number of ways—HSV, RGB, CMYK, and PMS are the most common. *HSV* stands for hue, saturation, and value, the three attributes common to all color. *RGB* stands for red, green, and blue, the additive primaries used for color television and color computer monitors. It has no direct correlation to subtractive color printed on paper. *CMYK* stands for cyan, magenta, yellow, and black; the process colors used in four-color printing. *PMS* stands for the Pantone Matching System, the same standardized ink matching system commonly used in color printing that is not four-color process.

A number of bit-map programs allow you to sketch in color on the screen (as opposed to the drawing programs, which allow you to specify color overlays for production art), and each has a different way of letting you specify and control color. The number of colors you see on a typical color monitor varies from the modest 256 colors that can be seen simultaneously on an 8-bit system, to more than 16 million simultaneous colors available on 24- and 32-bit systems. This so far exceeds the range of PMS colors, which have a fixed number of formulas, and of process colors, which progress in fixed increments of 5 to 10 percent, that the designer must keep the limitations of printing in mind when sketching on the screen. Many of the color paint programs allow you to work in one color system and then look at the color in other systems. If you sketch with PMS colors, for example, you can then choose CMYK and see process-color equivalents for the colors you have chosen. Many people enjoy working with PMS colors first, either because they are already familiar with these colors or because the PMS system offers such a pleasing range of colors from which to choose.

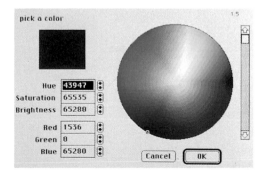

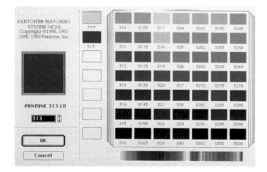

Most color software gives you several ways to specify and modify color, some of which relate directly to the way color is specified for the printed page. Shown here is the Apple Macintosh Color Picker menu (left) and a PMS color chooser (right).

COLOR VARIATIONS

When you sketch on screen, you must keep in mind the manner in which the sketch will be presented. If your screen sketch is to be presented on a client's screen, for example, it may look slightly different. Each screen has its own idiosyncrasies and may be adjusted differently. If you will be presenting your screen sketch or comp as slides or photographic prints, be aware that color may be affected by film type, exposure time, and film processing. The greatest difference arises when the screen sketch is converted to hard copy, such as a color printout. Color printers were created with business needs, rather than the needs of the designer, in mind, and what might be unimportant color variations to a business user can present major problems to a designer.

There are many color printers on the market, and each has its own idiosyncratic shifts in hue, value, and contrast. When you know in advance what kind of presentation format you will be using, you can adjust the color on the screen so that the presentation format best represents your design. Once you have established a system for presenting your work, you can anticipate these shifts and compensate for them in advance.

The image on the screen (top) has subtleties that the color printout (bottom) does not capture. In general, bright clear colors print well, but neutral and complex colors do not.

4

Although their purposes are similar, the techniques and materials used for sketches are considerably different than those used for comps. In sketches, elements are *indicated;* indication techniques are a kind of shorthand the designer develops to communicate the things they need to show on a typical layout. In comps, elements are *imitated* rather than indicated, that is, they look real to the viewer. One might think of a comp as a forgery of a printed piece. Whereas a comp could be mistaken for a printed piece, a sketch is always a sketch, however well its elements have been indicated.

In this section, techniques for indicating and comping typical layout elements are introduced. Indication techniques are presented first, followed by comping techniques. Computer-based techniques are introduced separately. Some computer-based techniques are used in combination with noncomputer techniques, and others are meant for use in place of the materials and techniques introduced in this section.

COMMUNICATING THE RIGHT MESSAGE

To be effective, sketches and comps must communicate the idea without distracting the viewer from that idea. This is true whatever the technology or the level of refinement. A design idea is communicated well only when the viewer thinks of the design rather than the techniques used to present it. Each element must be communicated with as little ambiguity as possible; for example, the viewer should perceive of a photo indication as being a sketch of a photograph and not confuse it with a drawing or an illustration; a title should be seen as typeset words, not as hand lettering.

4

A sketch or comp communicates more than a design idea; a well-executed sketch or comp also carries implicit messages—professionalism, craftsmanship, competence, planning ability, an understanding of the production processes that are to follow design, and a respect for the client's goals. A poorly executed sketch or comp may imply a different message—haphazard work habits, poor skills, the inability to plan ahead, and a lack of interest in or concern about the client's interests and goals. All of this affects the client's perception of the designer and influences the client's perception of the ideas themselves.

MAINTAINING A CONSISTENT LEVEL OF REFINEMENT

Whether working on a sketch or a comp, it is important that all of the elements are at the same level of refinement. When one element is more refined than another, or when the visualization is a hodgepodge of techniques, both rough and refined, the viewer will find it difficult to understand what is to be taken literally and what is to be overlooked. In a sketch, for example, the viewer is expected to ignore the inadvertent textures created by marker or pencil and the inaccuracies that arise from imprecise tools. In a comp, the viewer is being shown more and asked to imagine less, but even in the most refined comp, what the viewer sees cannot be taken completely literally.

Sketching and comping techniques are presented separately throughout this book, and the reader should retain this distinction when adapting techniques. The idea, then, is not to use the combination of techniques that are the most convenient to the designer, but to use the ones that are the most effective for presentation.

Sketching and comping enable the designer to test ideas by exploring them more precisely and in more detail. The designer should not begin sketches and comps, then, until he or she has developed coherent thumbnails from which to work. The process of creating sketches and comps will almost always suggest additional ideas, but the designer should not rely solely on inspiration at this level because it does not involve thinking about the design problem as a whole.

The impression that a good designer works completely spontaneously, without thought or planning, is a superficial one. Beginning designers should be wary of emulating the work patterns of those who have been designing for many years—preliminary thinking becomes so much a part of the process, and the design problems so familiar, that the experienced designer may no longer be conscious of the preliminary thinking and planning that occurs.

Before beginning the sketch or comp, the designer should take the time to assemble all of the materials that may be needed for underlays and have on hand the tools and materials that may be required. Attention should be paid to the work area as well; if the work area is clean and organized, the designer will have fewer distractions once the sketching or comping begins and will be able to focus only on design.

FORMAT

Plan the way in which the sketches or comps will be presented before you begin to work, rather than spending time later in trying to find a consistent way in which to present them. If, for example, you are working on sketches for a logo or symbol, it is advantageous to precut tracing paper in an appropriate format—six-inch squares or half-sized sheets, for example—and make a small folder or envelope in which to keep them. Prepare your underlays and choose your materials and tools accordingly. If you are showing comp layouts smaller than 8½-by-11 inches, you may wish to present them on a smaller mounting board than the 15-by-20-inch standard.

The appropriate scale for sketching depends on a number of factors, including the design, the formality of the presentation, the expectations of the client, and the money and time available for idea development. For some types of projects, half-sized sketches and comps are a good midpoint between thumbnails and comps in that they allow the designer to visualize ideas in a structured way without the investment in time required by full-sized sketches and comps. Half-sized sketches and comps are good alternatives when a client's budget is tight and does not allow for an appropriate amount of design development and visualization. For some projects, such as billboards, it is not feasible to work at actual size—sketches must be considerably smaller than actual size.

—SCALE AND PERCEPTION. Scale often affects our perception of a design. A small, tight sketch of a brochure, for example, may be appealing simply because of its scale. Business stationery (letterhead, business card, and envelope) is best presented at actual size because size is so important a factor in its design. Symbols such as logos and icons are often presented in a large size for impact, but care should be taken that the symbol be developed in a size typical of that in which it will appear. A common error in designing symbols is to work too far out of scale—the amount of detail we perceive, and shapes and their relationships, change dramatically at different scales. Something that is clearly an object in a large size, such as a bird, may become a blob in a small size. It is important, then, that in addition to the large-sized symbol shown, a typical size be presented as well. Detailed symbols may need to be drawn differently at different scales; the IBM logo, for example, has a different number of stripes for the dramatically different sizes in which it appears.

This half-sized comp of a brochure spread is one of several presented to show possible design directions. The client chose one for further refinement as a full-sized comp. *(West and Moravec)*

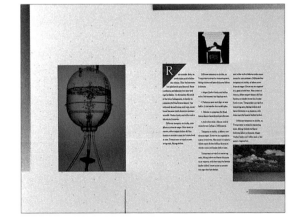

TEXT INDICATION

Text is type that is smaller than 14 points in size and is generally smaller than 12 points. It most typically appears on the page in columns, address blocks, and other elements, such as captions. The goal of text indication is to represent, quickly and consistently, the proportion, *color* (the shade of gray the text creates on the page), and texture of typeset text. Techniques commonly used in roughs for showing text, such as thick black lines, are inappropriate for indicating text in sketches, which are more refined and realistic. Good text indication will show such details as alignment, indents, bold and regular weights of type, and extra leading between paragraphs, as well as leading, point size, line length, justification, and overall color. Experiment with several techniques to find one that works best for you; evaluate your technique by comparing it for texture and color with the text sample you are representing. Whatever technique you use, it must be fast enough to allow you to work quickly, yet consistent enough to let you indicate large areas of text without significant changes in texture and color.

—REFERENCE UNDERLAYS. To indicate text specimens well, you need to use text as underlays. Working with a text underlay ensures a more believable pattern. Although many type specimen books include blocks of text for visual reference, they generally offer a limited range of options. Gather text specimens from ads, magazines, brochures, and other printed pieces so that you have more variety to work from. If you have access to a computer and a laser printer, you can create your own text underlays in a wide range of point sizes and leadings. In creating text underlays, keep in mind that the leading, point size, line length, and overall color are more critical than the exact typeface. Try to match the general proportions of the typeface you want to indicate, however. If the text underlay matches the specifications you intend to use in the final design, the underlay will provide you with an approximate character count (number of letters, spaces, etc.) for each layout, which will be useful when comparing layouts to each other and to final copy.

When indicating text, develop a technique that will enable you to match the overall color and texture of the text being indicated, to work quickly, and to be consistent over a large area. From left to right: the text underlay, double-line indication, line indication with a china marker, and three scribble techniques.

—TECHNIQUES. There are several common techniques for indicating text; experiment with them, then develop some techniques of your own. Text is commonly indicated with a fine-tipped marker, a drafting pen, or a soft black pencil, as shown in the examples. If the text is to be printed in color, use a marker or pencil in the appropriate color, or mix paint and use it in a ruling pen. If the text is to be reversed out of a darker color, use a ruling pen and paint so that your indication lines are crisp. (Although opaque white markers are available, they generally have tips that are too broad for text indication and may not be compatible with your other markers.) Using a ruling pen is generally faster and more effective than trying to color in the background around the text (see *Using a ruling pen* in section 3).

When a soft black pencil is used with a laser-printed underlay, the pressure from the pencil often causes some of the text to transfer to the back of the tracing paper, lending a more realistic detail.

In matching the color of the text you are tracing, keep in mind that photocopies and laser printing tend to be considerably darker than the text you are actually indicating. To make a crisp, justified margin, mask the edge of the column with Magic Plus tape or with frisket (see *Masking* in section 3).

Display type is typesetting that is 14 points and larger; it is most generally used for headlines, titles, and large initial letters (caps) at the beginning of text paragraphs. Unlike text type, which is only indicated, display type should consist of real letterforms in the appropriate words. In display sizes of type, even letterspacing is critical; the spaces between letters should be *optically* rather than *mechanically* balanced, that is, the distance between letters should look even as a whole, not just measure the same. It is worth taking a little extra time to work out any problems with spacing on the underlay before tracing the type onto the sketch.

—REFERENCE UNDERLAYS. Because the display type on a sketch should match the level of refinement of the other elements, using transfer lettering or laser-printed type directly on the sketch is inappropriate. Both of these forms of comping typesetting, however, are extremely useful as underlays. Trace type from a specimen sheet into the words and sizes you need for the underlay or use transfer lettering. If the transfer type is not the exact size required, enlarge or reduce it with a photocopier to fit your layout once you have transferred the letters into position. If you know that you will be making extreme changes in size (over 25 percent), space the type with the actual size in mind. The spaces between letters do not scale at the same rate as the letterforms, so large type that is to be made much smaller should have looser-than-desired spacing, and small type that is being enlarged should have tighter-than-desired spacing. When you are scaling type photographically, remember that you are indicating something to be typeset; work with point sizes that are available to your typesetting system.

In tracing display type, use a straightedge to trace the tops and bottoms of letters so that the letters will have a uniform height. The remainder of each letter can generally be traced freehand.

INDICATE

—BASELINES. Lines of type sit on a *baseline*. Draw a baseline before you begin tracing type for your underlay and before you begin using transfer type. Some letters—those with curved bottoms—sit *optically* rather than mechanically along a baseline, that is, part of the curve extends below the baseline so that the letter as a whole will *look* aligned. If you are using desktop technology for your underlay, or are having type set, the type will be aligned correctly. If you are using transfer lettering, use the small guidelines provided on the transfer sheet to ensure that the letters are aligned on the baseline correctly. It is sometimes useful to draw a light pencil baseline on your sketch as well; you may want to draw this line on the back of the tracing paper on which you are working rather than on the front so that you can erase it later without smearing any of the other marker or pencil.

—HEIGHTS AND WIDTHS. The most common errors in drawing display type are inconsistent letter heights and stroke widths. To avoid these errors, tape a preprinted sheet of square-grid paper to your board or pad, then tape your type underlay on top of it. Next, tape your sketch in position so that the type and grid are square to the edges of the paper. To keep letter heights even, first position a straightedge along the very tops of the letters, then draw a horizontal line only where you see a flat stroke ending and a dot where you see tips and at the tops of curves. Do the same with the base of each line of type. Connect the dots and lines; you can probably do this freehand unless the typeface is one that is mechanically constructed, such as Avant Garde or Futura. As you draw, keep the tip of your pen on the black of the letter rather than on its edge to avoid making the type bolder.

The tool you use to trace with will depend on the color and size of your type elements—you might use markers, a technical pen, or a ruling pen and paint for tracing type. No matter what tool you use, draw the outline first with a fine tip; if the type is bold, fill in the letters with a broader tip. If you are using markers, test the fine and broad tips for a color match before you draw, even if you are using black. It is more difficult to get a crisp edge with colored pencils than with marker, paint, or ink.

The style and character of this public service message (right) was established by this simple marker sketch (left), and despite minor changes made during the production phase of the project, they look quite similar. *(Ed Seubert)*

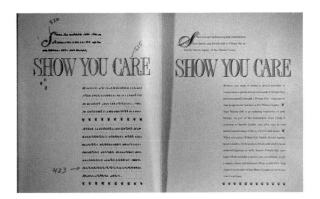

Photographs for a design may or may not already exist. Existing photographs simplify the visualization task because the designer does not also need to compose the photograph. The designer can transform any photograph in a number of ways: photos can be *cropped* (trimmed to create a different composition); screened back so that they appear as ghost images; or shot as line art or with special-effects screens. Black-and-white photographs might also be printed as duotones or in a color other than black. Color photographs can sometimes be printed in black and white; black-and-white photographs might be hand tinted in colors. The way in which the photograph is used is shown with a photo indication.

—REFERENCE MATERIALS. If a photograph is to scale, it can be used as an underlay for the photo indication. If possible, however, use a photocopy as an underlay instead so that the photo can be next to your paper for reference as you sketch. Once you have developed an ability to copy the shapes and values you see, the photocopy can be any size. If the photograph does not exist, try to find existing photographs to draw from. If you cannot find something appropriate, you may need to create a collage of elements from your scrap files.

—TECHNIQUES. The most important thing to remember is that you are indicating a photograph, not drawing. Copy the shapes you see on the photograph, no matter how meaningless or insignificant they seem, and avoid preconceived notions about the shapes of the objects in the photograph. Never outline the subjects in a photo. You are drawing only the pattern of light, color, and shadow, not the objects themselves. If you need some lines as drawing guides, put them on an underlay rather than on the sketch itself.

Establish the value range by first putting in the darkest values. Include even the smallest, seemingly insignificant areas and shapes. When you have put in the darkest values, your photo indication may look more like a Dalmatian dog than the subject of the photograph, but as you add the medium values the subject will emerge, just as it has in the photograph. A photocopy helps create the value pattern for you, and it may seem a quick and easy substitute for a drawn photo indication, especially if it is on the same kind of paper as the rest of the sketch, but it will not have the same character and quality as the other elements in your sketch.

TOM UPTON

To establish the value range and to define the shapes in a photo indication, trace the darkest values first.

Once the value range has been established, proportions and positions of elements have been established as well, and it is relatively easy to add the middle values. Use marker for solid darks and crisp edges. To indicate soft edges, use black or colored pencil. When very dark elements have soft edges, use marker first to establish value, then apply pencil to soften edges.

When you add pencil shading, make sure you have a soft pad of paper under the paper you are drawing on. Pencil picks up the texture of whatever is under the paper; the more even the padding, the easier to apply color evenly. (You can use this to your advantage when you want to add a specific texture.)

—MASKING VERSUS ASSEMBLY. You may wish to create the photo indication on a separate sheet of paper rather than work directly on your layout, particularly if it is a complex one. Work on the same kind of paper as the layout to create the photo indication, draw a pencil line marking the trim of the photo indication, and make sure you work freely beyond that line so that the color, stroke, and values are consistent. There is no need to work carefully along the edges because you will create clean edges when you trim the photo indication. During final assembly, trim the photo indication to size, apply a light coat of spray adhesive to the back, and stick it in position.

If you choose to work on the same sheet of paper as the rest of your layout, mask the edges of the photo indication before you begin with Magic Plus tape to keep the edges crisp. Note, however, that some markers bleed under the tape so test before you begin. Work quickly along edges; begin marker strokes on the tape and draw strokes away from, rather than toward, the tape. Remove the tape when you are done. Do not draw a box around the photo indication unless you intend to print a border. If you intend to print a border, consider whether it will touch the image. If it will not, draw the border directly on the sketch, then mask or assemble with a space between the border and the photo.

In this duotone indication (top), the color photograph (bottom) was first photocopied to establish values, then tinted with colored pencils to add the second color.

TOM UPTON

—INDICATING DUOTONES. Work as though you are creating a black-and-white photo, then add a subtle layer of color over the sketch with a colored pencil, following the same dark-to-light pattern established with the blacks and grays. White highlights remain white. If it will not smear the marker and pencil already on the paper, you may want to use a pale marker instead. On tracing paper, you can add color to the back side as well. If the duotone is comprised of an overall tint screen with a halftone printed over it, put in the background color first, either with a marker or a marker sprayer. A duotone need not be printed in black—some duotones are printed in two colors. Work the same way as for a black-and-white photo indication to create values, beginning with the darkest color.

—INDICATING COLOR PHOTOGRAPHS. Make an underlay either by tracing the shapes in the photo or by making a photocopy. Use black marker for the darkest areas, even if they are not quite black in the photo; value and tone can be adjusted by layering pencil over a marker base. When the colors in the photo are rich and saturated, add values first, just as in a black-and-white photo indication, then add hue. Use the marker-and-pencil techniques described in section 3.

In these sketches for a small brochure, the designer indicated a photo of a musical instrument in the first, a photo of a paper sculpture in the second, and a table-top photo in the third. The photo indication was part of the overall concept for the brochure. *(Russell Leong Design)*

INDICATING ILLUSTRATIONS

Illustrations include *technical* illustrations, such as diagrams and precision drawings, *line* drawings, watercolor *renderings*, graphs—in short, any nontypographic element that is drawn, whether it is by hand or by computer. *Spot* (small) illustrations are very small and are often added only for decoration. Whenever possible, give enough information so that the viewer can differentiate a photo indication from an illustration indication.

—REFERENCE MATERIALS. Existing illustrations can be used as underlays or resized on a photocopier, and the photocopies can be used as underlays. If illustrations do not exist, you will need to compose them and capture the essence of the technique you want to have in the actual illustration. Layouts, proportions, and overall values should be worked out on a sheet of scrap paper; this sketch can act as an underlay. You may be able to find an example of an illustration that is similar in size and shape, however, since illustrators have highly individual techniques, you may need to choose the illustrator before you do the indication, so that you have a specific style to communicate.

—TECHNIQUE. Large illustrations, such as paintings, are among the most difficult elements to indicate. A poor indication detracts from the presentation; a good indication may be as time consuming to create as the illustration itself. Unless you have excellent illustration skills, do not try to create the illustration; instead, capture the general character and color of the illustration you would like to see created. It is useful to work from samples of a specific illustrator's work so that you capture the feeling of his or her style. Do not give way to the temptation of doing the illustration itself; in the sketch you are indicating an illustration, not illustrating. Illustration is a separate step in the design process and deserves separate thought and attention. When you are indicating spot illustrations of line drawings, a few lines that capture the shape and color of the spot illustration may suffice; if the spot illustration exists, use it as an underlay. Any illustration indication that represents a technically precise drawing should be drawn carefully on the sketch, using straightedges and masking as called for. You may find it expedient to use the same assembly technique for indicating illustrations as described for indicating photographs.

Accent color is any small element that will be printed in a color other than black, such as a *rule* (line) or bar, border, initial capital, or logo. Rules and other fine detail can be added with a marker or a ruling pen and paint. Use a coloring book approach for larger elements: draw an outline first with a thin line, then fill it in, making sure the outline and the filled color match in hue and saturation. The technique you use for color accents will depend very much on the specific sketching materials you are using (see *Color* in section 3). If you are showing a detailed accent, such as a decorated color band, draw the outline of the smaller shapes with the color of the larger; for example, a red zigzag line on a green bar can be outlined in green, then filled in with red.

—COLOR FIELDS. A color *field* is any large area of color, such as a background. When color is a dominant part of a design, think in terms of printed color—if you are indicating four-color process printing, for example, some colors will not be obtainable. If you are indicating Pantone colors, you are ruling out four-color photographs unless you are printing on larger than a four-color press or plan multiple press runs. Using color references, such as tint screen charts and PMS swatchbooks, help you think beyond your basic marker and pencil palette.

—TECHNIQUE. When you are filling in large areas of color with marker, the specific paper and marker combination is important, and it is critical to test before you begin working. On some paper surfaces markers blend quickly; on others, markers leave stripes. To get an even overall value and texture you will need to add color in layers, saturating the paper until it bleeds. Along edges, however, you want a minimum of bleed. Use marker to establish the general value and hue of an area; then, once the marker has dried, use colored pencil over the marker to even out the color and adjust value and hue. Pencil can be used to lay down an area of color if the value is light, if you have developed enough control to work with even strokes, and if the texture of the pencil does not distract from what you are indicating.

If you work with pencil exclusively, build up an overall color gradually by laying down one layer of pencil atop another, working in even, parallel strokes. Do not press so hard with the pencil that the paper fibers are stretched and the paper surface is deformed. Rather than working on a thick pad of paper to ensure an even texture, work either on a thinner backing of soft paper or on a few sheets of smooth, hard paper. The firm backing will help keep the paper surface intact.

Color accents, such as broad rules, can be created separately and then trimmed and applied to a sketch or comp.

—GRADUATED COLOR. If you practice using colored pencil and have a light touch, you will be able to make a relatively small field of graduated color quite easily. Use a soft pad of paper under your sketch as you work. A marker sprayer may be a good alternative to pencil but only after you have practiced laying down even, overlapping strokes. Mask the area to be sprayed carefully. Use frisket for complex shapes; if the edges are straight, use Magic Plus tape to mask the edge. Cover the rest of the sketch with tracing paper taped in place.

—TEXTURES. If you are planning a textured surface for the printed piece, your sketch will be more interesting if you indicate the texture on your sketch, even if the texture is very subtle. Lay down a base color with marker, then put the sketch over an appropriately textured surface and add texture by rubbing the area with pencil. If you are working on tracing paper, add subtle texture to the back rather than the front.

—LOGOS AND LOGOTYPES. Most clients supply the designer with their logos and logotypes for reference; these can be used as underlays. Although most logos and logotypes appear in different sizes on different kinds of products, most companies follow a corporate standard that dictates specific sizes and positions for specific kinds of printed pieces. Whenever possible, check with the client about such requirements as size, positioning, and color. Use a marker or a ruling pen to add the logo or logotype. Because this element is one with which the client is particularly familiar, it is worth a little extra care in detailing, but it should remain in character with the rest of the sketch.

—DIE CUTTING. If you are sketching a die cut piece, such as a presentation folder or package, sketch it as it will appear assembled rather than showing it flat, as the camera-ready art will be. If it is three-dimensional, you may need to show several views.

—EMBOSSING. Do not try to emboss the surface of the sketch, but rather indicate the embossing by drawing the light and shadow of it. This is generally achieved by using the shape of the embossed image as an underlay, then imagining a single light source, such as one from the top and right. Keep in mind that shadows will relate to the value of the area being embossed; for example, an embossing on light paper would not have a black shadow. If you are proposing that the printed piece be on a high-gloss paper surface, you may also want to indicate highlights, either with pencil or paint that is a few shades lighter than the field in which the embossing appears. To show a register embossing, add color, then the embossing light and shadow.

A surprisingly realistic embossing indication can be created by drawing a few simple lines defining highlights and shadow. This one, drawn on tracing paper, was presented with gray paper behind it.

Whatever the tool or technology you are using, your goals for sketching are the same—showing your ideas for a design to their best advantage. A sketch must retain a balance between spontaneity and accuracy; working with a computer encourages accuracy but may interfere with spontaneity until you are familiar with using it. You can stay in sketching mode and encourage spontaneity to some extent by using a paint program rather than a more exacting drawing program. The kind of program you use, however, will depend on what you are doing.

—COMBINING TOOLS. Many people who begin using computers feel that they must limit themselves to the computer for all phases of visualization and design. No single tool or technology is best for everything—learn to mix tools and techniques to get the effects you want. It is appropriate to include the computer in your toolbox but only if it provides you with additional capabilities. When it does not, use whatever tool or technique you find more appropriate. Whether sketching, comping, or producing camera-ready art, choose the tool, or combination of tools, that work best and fastest to give the best result for a given situation.

For this quarter-page ad, type elements were created on a computer and laser printed onto tracing paper (left), then photo indications and color were added. This is faster and more effective than indicating type by hand.
(West and Moravec)

When using a paint program for layout, work in a reduced size so that your page size does not use more than half the screen and is not larger than half its actual size. Draw the page frame to proportion; if possible, make this a dotted line so that it will appear gray when printed out. Set aside part of the screen as a work area in which to create elements for your layout.

Create the key elements you will be using and keep them in reserve in the work area, making copies of them as you need them. Elements you will be reusing frequently, such as the page frame, should go in your scrapbook, if your system has one, for easy retrieval if you inadvertently damage an element as you work. To work most efficiently, set up a master sketch file that contains your edited patterns and page frame; rename it as a new file for each new project.

—INDICATING TEXT. Most programs will allow you to edit patterns. Edit several patterns that you will not be using for other purposes so that they have the character of text and represent different point sizes and leadings. If you cannot edit patterns, use horizontal stripes. Create a column of each pattern in your work area; if you will be using unjustified text, make the right edge of the column irregular.

—INDICATING DISPLAY TYPE. Display type must be set as real words; in a paint program, the letters will be *jagged* (stair-stepped curves and angles rather than smooth lines), but this will not interfere with using them in sketches. It is likely that your display type will need respacing once you have *entered* (typed) it; do this with your selection tool, a letter at a time, much as you would if you were pasting type down letter by letter on paper. It is generally best to create display type elements in the work area, then copy them into position on layouts. (If you are working with a color system and creating type on a colored background, you may need to create a color field outside the page frame on which to create the letters, then put them into position.)

These thumbnails show ideas for the first page of a bulletin. The low resolution of the paint program used to create them does not interfere with the communication of the ideas.

—PHOTOGRAPHS AND ILLUSTRATION. If you are sketching in a paint program, your working size will be small. To indicate a photograph or illustration, a *gesture sketch* is often adequate—this captures the main shapes, colors, values, and composition. If high-resolution scanning technology is available and it is appropriate to spend the extra time and effort needed to scan photographs into your system, more refined visual representations of photographs and illustrations can be achieved.

—OTHER ELEMENTS. Embossings can be shown in the same way they are on a paper sketch—by drawing in shadows and highlights. Logos and logotypes should be sketched, matching overall shape as closely as possible. It may not be possible to indicate subtle textures and tints if you are working on a black-and-white system.

—COMBINING TOOLS. Unless you have a very good color printer at your disposal, your printouts will be in black-and-white. If you are using the printout only for the type, page frame, and black elements, an effective technique is to print the whole layout first, including all of the elements, for use as an underlay. Print a second version on tracing paper showing only the elements you want from the computer, then draw other elements, such as photo indications, using the first printout as a positioning underlay.

An embossing is indicated on the screen much as it is on paper.
(Randy Moravec Design)

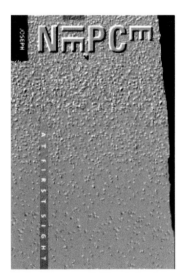

These sketches for a book cover
and chapter opening are the
equivalent of marker sketches,
in that they were done to explore
a range of design directions. No
specific details about type, grids, or
content were made at this stage in
the process. *(Randy Moravec Design)*

Unlike paint programs, which always print at *screen* resolution, drawing programs adopt *printer* resolution; if you use a laser printer, your sketch will look much more refined than one created in a paint program. The tools in a drawing program are considerably different than those in a paint program. Most allow more precision and give you the option of working with mathematical rather than visual scaling and positioning of elements. Some drawing programs, such as Aldus Freehand, allow you to edit patterns just as in a paint program. Unlike a paint program, however, when you draw a field of pattern, such as a column of text, you are actually making a window in which the pattern will appear. Although it may seem that you are changing the position of a column-of-text pattern, you are really moving only the window. You will need to size and position your text pattern window so that part of it will not be cut off at the top or bottom.

Just as with a paint program, set up a page frame and create elements outside it. If it is possible to have more than one window open at a time, you can use one window for your page and another for the elements you create. Work no larger than half size. Some drawing programs will allow you to import and print scans along with the drawing, but some will not. If you will be using scanned images for photographs and illustrations, you may find it more convenient to use a layout program instead of a drawing program. Many layout programs have basic drawing tools, but most do not offer fill patterns.

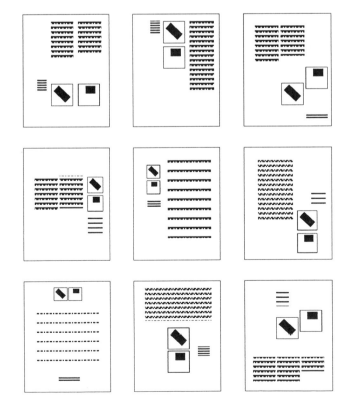

Although it may seem obvious to use layout software for sketching layouts, a layout program may offer so much "reality" that the designer is confronted with too many detailed decisions too soon. A layout program, however appropriate for a tight comp or camera-ready art, is distracting when the designer is first exploring ideas and indicating elements. One way in which a layout program can be used effectively for sketching is to work at a reduced scale; some software does this better than others. PageMaker, for example, allows you to work at a small scale and still see elements such as text as indications. Programs that use a block-out approach, in which boxes represent elements, do not give visual feedback about the color and texture of elements and are inappropriate for sketching ideas. Because layout programs are integration programs as well, they are the best choice when you need to combine elements created in several other programs.

—PROCEDURE. Use a greeking file for text and work in a small size—one that will allow you to fit the entire image on the screen at the same time. Always view the layout at a reduced size in order to keep a *Gestalt* view (overview of the whole) and do not get caught up in details. Never print the layout at actual size. If you are using PageMaker or another layout program that allows you to change parameters quickly, you can copy the elements on one page, add a page, and paste the elements on the new page, then change their specifications, proportions, sizes, and positions. A scan of a photograph, for example, can be recropped and rescaled; the line length, leading, justification, size, and position of text can be changed easily as well.

Some layout software allows you to change the way in which text is indicated on the screen when viewed at a reduced size; if the text does not have the character and texture you want, use a striped pattern as text indication. Page layout software has the advantage of letting you establish a grid on which to create your layout sketches. Even if you do not use the layout program to generate the entire layout, consider using it to print out thumbnail-sized grids for use as underlays. Once you have created a series of layouts with the software, print them out in thumbnail size, or as 50 percent printouts. Programs such as PageMaker allow you to print thumbnails of your layouts at several sizes; the size is controlled by the number of thumbnails per page you specify.

In these sketches of a technical brochure, created in a layout program, a draft of the proposed text was used rather than text indication. This provided the client and writer with useful feedback before the text was completed and approved. *(Randy Moravec Design)*

To get the widest range of ideas, and to see the widest possible interpretation of forms when developing a symbol, it is important to work with many different tools and techniques. Sketching with a paint or drawing program allows you to do some things more quickly and with more precision than sketching by hand; for example, circles and squares can be drawn with relative precision and elements can be multiplied, rotated, modified, and manipulated with relative ease. Each type of software has its strengths and weaknesses, and each can become distracting because of the range of possibilities offered.

Because the computer has as much influence on the overall look of the design as a paintbrush or other drawing tool, ideas developed from scratch with specific software are likely to have tell-tale characteristics. If this is not desirable, develop specific ideas in thumbnail form before you begin and use software only for refining and modifying ideas.

If you are using the software to generate ideas, make this a separate step in the design process, evaluating these ideas along with those generated other ways. Keep in mind that variation and quality come from the designer and not from the software.

These thumbnail sketches illustrating the concept of convergence were created using a drawing program. Some of these ideas were sketched on paper first; others were inspired by the capabilities of the software used. *(West and Moravec)*

In creating a comp, the designer's goal is to create something that could be mistaken for an actual printed piece from a few feet away (the normal viewing distance for a comp). A comp is intended to represent the designer's idea for a printed piece in such a way that the viewer thinks of what he or she sees not as a sketch or assemblage of parts but as a manifestation of the printed piece itself. Little should be left to the viewer's imagination. The viewer, for example, should automatically think of a photo indication as a photograph, rather than as a marker sketch or a photocopy; he or she should view display type as typesetting, not hand lettering.

A good comp should not require an explanation—it should visually communicate to the viewer in such a way that the viewer clearly sees the design. Each element must be as unambiguous as possible. If the appropriate level of realism isn't achieved, the viewer is likely to be distracted from the design because he or she will be trying to interpret the technique used. A comp requires considerably more planning and preparation than a sketch, and it is likely that considerably more preliminary development will have taken place before the comping than before sketching. Once the planning and preparation are done, however, the execution of one or more comps is relatively swift. For the experienced designer, comping may be much less time consuming than sketching.

This comp (right) was so carefully planned that the design changed very little during the production phase. *(Paige Johnson Design)*

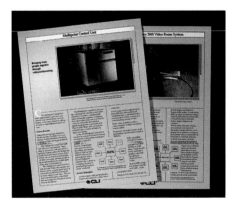

The best and most efficient method for creating comps is to use an assembly, or *collage*, method in which all of the parts are created separately, then combined into a final layout. Illustrators often use this method on complex pieces for many of the same reasons as a designer: you can work on several versions of an element, then decide which provides the best combination; you do not need to begin everything again if you make a mistake; and you can work with the most appropriate papers and films for each part. As a general rule, create elements separately whenever possible.

—VISIBLE EDGE. A comp should never have a patchwork appearance. The viewer should never be aware that an assembly technique has been used, so not all of the elements in a layout can be assembled—some element must be created directly on the comp. Only those elements that would have a visible edge anyway, such as the edge created by a change in color, should be included. A photograph, for example, has a visible edge—there is a difference in color and value between it and the background—so it can be created separately and adhered to the comp. An area of text and display type, however, must be created directly on the background. Plan the elements that will be created directly on the comp first and create them in position. Don't trim the comp to the final size until all of the elements, especially the elements that bleed, have been put in place.

This comp of a direct-mail piece (left) was created with cut paper and photocopying. Because the photocopying was done directly on the comping paper, there are no edges visible on the comp that are not also visible on the printed piece (right).
(Henry Brimmer)

CREATING A MASTER

The elements in a comp have often been created by different techniques or have been gathered from a variety of sources, but to use some of these directly on the comp would give a patchwork appearance. So that the comp appears seamless, elements should be pasted up on a separate white board as camera-ready art to make a master. (Remember that the camera-ready art is line art—the camera will only produce black and white and will see everything as either black or white.) The master can be used as camera-ready art for custom transfers, photostats, film positives or negatives, and as the original for photocopying onto comping papers. Create elements separately when possible, then add them to the master. If, for example, if you are using a transfer-lettered headline for an ad, transfer the type onto a sheet of paper, then paste or tape the paper onto the master. This will allow you to modify its position later and to cut the lines of type apart to space and align them differently.

If you have added a number of pieces to the master, you may need to make a photostat or very good quality photocopy of the master before photocopying onto comping paper so that the cut edges do not show.

—COMPUTER-GENERATED MASTERS. If you are using a computer to generate the type for your comp, work the same way—keep headline and text as separate elements to be rearranged and print out variations. As a general rule, any paper that will feed through a photocopier will also feed through a laser printer, because the laser printer uses the same electrostatic printing technology. Some people get better results when they print their computer-generated elements onto white paper and then cut and paste them just as they do other elements, rather than arrange them on screen.

These cards are comps. Image-setter paper output was used to comp the fronts of the cards. Image-setter film negative output was laminated to paper on which color had been applied, so that it would show through the clear areas on the film.

This lamination was used as a master to create high-quality color copies for the card backs. Card fronts and backs were laminated with spray adhesive. *(Yuki Nishinaka)*

MARK SCHWARTZ

—TRANSFER TEXT, such as that made by Letraset, is available in a limited range of sizes and styles and in white as well as black. This is useful for small amounts of text when detailing and color are not critical and when the range of sizes and styles available suit the design. Transfer text works in the same way as other transfer products—the element to be transferred is positioned, then rubbed with a burnisher to make the transfer.

Use an underlay of column guides to position text rather than drawing guidelines directly on your comp. The justified left margin of the transfer text should be used as the justified left edge of your column. Because your columns will probably be narrower than the columns provided on the transfer sheet, place a strip of Magic Plus tape along your right margin before you transfer the text so that lines remain the appropriate length and no stray letters go beyond the edge of the column. If you are indicating a ragged right margin, transfer the lines of type to allow different line lengths. If you are indicating a justified column, lines of text may end with partial letters. You may need to add letters to the ends of some of the lines so that they meet the edge of your column. Do this carefully so that the letters align with the line of type.

Transfer text tends to have a limited shelf life; old text does not transfer consistently. Make sure to test before you transfer onto your comp. Practice to get the right amount of pressure—the tendency is often to rub too hard, which not only stretches the plastic carrier of the transfer sheet but dents the surface of your comp. Sometimes it is more practical to transfer the text onto a master so that broken letters can be touched up and margins corrected, then photocopied onto the comp.

—FOUND TEXT, such as text printed in magazines, ads, and brochures, is a low-budget alternative to transfer text. The major drawback of found text is that it is set in real words rather than in greeking, and the text may be inappropriate or distracting. Because of this, the client's existing ads and brochures, or printed pieces that relate to the same topic, are generally better sources than advertising text. To use found text for a comp, you will need to create a paste-up that can be used as a master. When you make the master, you may be able to rearrange or edit the text so that it becomes more like greeking.

Draw your columns and positioning guides on an underlay, paste the text into position, and photocopy it onto the paper you are using for your comp. If the paper you are using does not accept photocopier toner well or will not feed through the machine, there are two alternatives: make a film positive, which can be used as an overlay so that the comping paper shows through, or have a custom transfer made of the text. Before you use found text in a comp, make sure you know how to specify it, and check to see that the typeface (or something very similar) is available on the typesetting technology that will be used for the camera-ready art.

—TYPESETTING. Many commercial typesetters have greeking on file and can set greeking text to your specifications. Use this just as you would found text—paste it into position and then photocopy it or order a film positive. Some desktop publishing services offer a wide variety of typefaces, and can set type to your specifications as well, but be sure that they can follow specifications, can kern the text appropriately, and will attend to such typesetting details as the evenness of the rag and the texture of justified columns. If you have a computer and the appropriate fonts and software, set greeking yourself and laser print it onto the paper you are using for your comp. If the paper you are using does not accept laser toner well or will not feed through the printer, order a film positive or have a custom transfer made of the text.

—CUSTOM TRANSFERS. When text is to be printed in color or is to be lighter than the background on which it will appear, order custom transfers of your text. You will need to create master art of your text. Transfer text, found text, and text generated by a computer are all acceptable as master art, but keep in mind that the quality of the type on your master is very close to what you will get as a custom transfer; any flaws you see on your master art will appear on the transfer as well. Because of resolution, desktop-generated text in very small point sizes will need to be printed out on a Linotronic image setter rather than laser printed, but laser printing is acceptable as a master for most other text. Keep in mind that laser-printed text is considerably bolder than the same text printed out on a Linotronic. If you want your comp to show text weight correctly, you will need to use Linotronic output. When you apply the text to your comp, use a minimum of pressure and the broad surface of your burnisher so that you do not dent the surface of your comp.

Text printed with a laser printer (right) is considerably heavier than text printed on an image setter (left).

Printing was from
ment. Not merely t
production; for the
was the first compl
and the movable t

Printing was fron
ment. Not merely t
production; for the
was the first compl
and the movable t

Whereas text is seen primarily as a texture on a comp and can be set in greeking, display type will need to be set in words that convey an appropriate message—the viewer will expect to read it. The words used determine the shape and texture of the display type at least as much as the specifications, so the correct copy should be used whenever possible. If the exact copy is not available, the designer should show a likely number of words—a different layout and point size is possible if a headline is one word, for example, than if the headline is a twelve-word phrase.

—TRANSFER TYPE is one of the fastest and easiest methods to use for display type. Transfer type provides the designer with a great deal of control over the spacing of the letters, a critical factor in setting display type, because one letter is applied at a time. It is wise to do a rough tracing of the display type first. The rough is a dry run; once the display type is traced and any spacing problems inherent in the particular combination of typeface and words being used have been resolved, the rough can be used as an underlay to confirm positioning on the comp.

If it is obvious to the viewer that you have used transfer type, you have used it incorrectly. The most common errors in using transfer lettering are tilted letters and uneven baselines. If you apply the type letter by letter to your comp, take care that you do not tilt the transfer sheet; use the baseline indicators on the transfer sheet to check alignment. Whenever possible, transfer display type onto a master first, then photocopy it onto the comp—once all of the letters are in place on the master, any imperfections in spacing or alignment in the display type can be fixed before the type goes on the comp. Another way to preview spacing before the transfer type is put on the layout is to use the Letraset Word Positioning System, in which the letters are transferred onto the Word Positioning strips first. The strips of paper in this system allow you to set a line of type at a time; if you want to set several lines, you will need to buy film/paper sets in sheets rather than in the more commonly available strips. Once spacing and alignment are adjusted, the lettering can be transferred onto the comp.

This newsletter design (left) began with conventional thumbnails (right) and includes many of the ideas explored during the comping phase of the project (next page). *(Mark Anderson Design)*

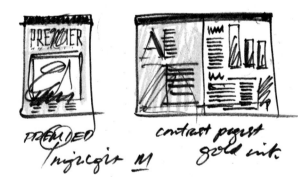

The computer provided the designer
with immediate feedback about typesetting and offered flexibility and precision
that would have been more difficult to
achieve with conventional tools and
techniques. It was particularly appropriate to develop these comps on a computer because type was so critical a part
of the design. *(Mark Anderson Design)*

—COLORED TRANSFER TYPE. If you are using the Word Positioning System, you can color white letters before you transfer them to the film by using a marker sprayer, such as a Letrajet. White custom transfers can be used with the Word Positioning System and colored as well. Apply color in a slow, continuous, back-and-forth motion of overlapping paths rather than in random fashion. Do not try to build up color all at once, but apply it in layers. It is easy to mix colors by respraying with a second or third color, but beware of adding too much color—if the backing paper is saturated with color, the color often transfers onto the film along with the type. Allow the marker color to dry thoroughly before you complete the transfer process. Marker sprayers allow you to apply color to only part of a letter; for example, color can be graduated from bottom to top so that the bottoms of the letters have full color and the tops of the letters fade to white.

When you use a marker sprayer, make sure that the can of compressed air is room temperature. As air is expelled from the can, the temperature of the contents gets so cold that ice forms on the outside of the can, the air is emitted unevenly, and the color splatters rather than sprays onto the paper.

—CUSTOM TRANSFERS may be a better choice than tinted letters when you are matching a specific color or if the color of the display type must match other color elements on the page, such as text or a logo. Create master art of your display type just as you want it to appear on the transfer sheet, and include any other elements you want to have the same color on the comp.

—CREATING A MASTER. The display type on your master can be generated a number of ways—for example, desktop technology, transfer lettering, or typesetting. Once you have created a master, it can be used not only for custom transfers, but also for photostats and both black-and-white and color photocopies. If you are making photocopies, test to see that the cut edges on the master will not show on the photocopy. If they do, have a stat or a high-quality photocopy made first, and eliminate any unwanted lines or marks. Use this cleaned-up copy as the master. Photocopies can be made directly onto your comp paper. If you are making color photocopies, however, keep in mind that many colors do not reproduce accurately and that the color of the paper is likely to influence your results. Be prepared for trial and error.

—COLOR PRINTERS. If you have generated your type on a desktop system, you may wish to print it in color. Although color printing technology has improved significantly, do not expect it (or any technology) to be foolproof. Although there is always some shift in color when moving from one technology and media to another, color printing systems tend to be designed for business use and not for recreating subtle colors accurately. Just as with color copiers, be prepared for trial and error to get the exact color you want.

To develop these comps for a type package wrapper, students ordered typesetting and created camera-ready masters for photocopying. The large type elements were set on a Macintosh. *(Barbara Cox, Romney Hudson, and Becky Fishbach)*

PHOTOGRAPHS

Photographs show more than mere subject matter; a photograph on a comp should be carefully planned so that the photo comp reflects the color, composition, and level of abstraction the designer intends for the final piece. Rather than simply applying a copy of a standard publicity photograph of a client's product to the comp, for example, use it as a point of departure for developing a photo comp that shows color characteristics such as saturation and hue, compositional symmetry, distance from the product (a close-up of a mundane product can become an exciting abstract design element), and other such visual information. Because the comp is for visual impact, such details are more important than merely using accurate subject matter. The designer may often spend as much time planning key photographs as he or she spends planning the layout in which they will appear.

In this exercise, the student matched the hues and values of the photograph so closely with marker and pencil that the indication can scarcely be differentiated from the photograph itself. *(Judy Mason)*

—TIGHT MARKER/PENCIL INDICATIONS. If you have developed some proficiency in creating photo indications, you can apply this skill to tight indications for comps. Photo indications on a comp must be more realistic and better detailed than photo indications on a sketch. If there are many black areas in the photograph, you may wish to begin with a black-and-white photocopy. Make sure, however, that the whiteness of the paper used in the indications is not brighter than the white of the paper on the comp itself. You may want to copy onto marker or layout paper rather than the white bond paper typically used in copiers. Marker sprayers used with frisket masks will allow you to tone specific areas evenly without disturbing the toner. Apply marker and pencil as described in section 3. When you are working only in black-and-white, take care that the blacks you use are the same shade of black. Blacks vary in hue from browns to blues; grays vary as well. Warm and cool blacks and grays mixed together produce a richness that cannot be achieved on the printed page unless warm and cool blacks are printed as duotones. So that neither of you is disappointed by the printed piece, you and the client need to understand that the richness achieved from two tones of black will not be achieved by printing one color of black.

PHOTO COLLAGES When a single found photograph does not provide the elements or composition you want to show in your comp, found photographic elements can often be combined to create a photo collage. The photo collage shows the intended proportions, colors, subjects, and composition. Care must be taken that the final image created can be shot with a camera; photo collages can often become collage illustrations instead, requiring multiple shots and extensive lab work during the production phase, which may exceed the budget allowed. In a photo collage, a background in one photo can be replaced with a background from another or by a piece of colored paper that matches your color scheme. Areas can be masked and tinted with a marker sprayer. Used carefully, the photo collage technique offers considerably more flexibility than stock photographs alone.

A photo collage should generally be used as a master, to be photostated or photocopied so that it appears to be one piece. Black-and-white photo collages often need to be shot as halftones. Anticipate color inaccuracies in reproducing color photo collages; detailed photographs, such as scenes and vases of flowers, tend to reproduce more successfully than photographs with a single, close-up subject, such as a portrait or a close-up detail of a product, particularly when subtle coloring is involved.

—USING FOUND PHOTOGRAPHS. *Found* photographs are those that already exist in use, such as those from catalogs, magazines, brochures, and other printed pieces. It has been common practice in the field to use found photographs "as is;" partly as a result of this practice, some designers often do not think through the photographic elements in their design as thoroughly or as creatively as they do the other elements. When using found photographs, such as the photographs found in magazines, keep in mind that these are generally copyright protected and have been commissioned by other designers for other clients. This may preclude their use in your final printed piece. Photographs in *stock* catalogs, however, are existing photographs that are available for use—"in stock"—and your client can purchase the right to use them for a specific purpose. Most stock-photography vendors provide catalogs of their stock; in addition to being useful as reference, these catalogs generally provide a wide range of subjects to use as a point of departure for photo comps. Another bonus is that some stock-photo companies are now making these photos available as scans as well, so that designers working on computers do not have to spend time on the intermediate processes of putting a printed photograph into digital form.

Photographic elements from a company's existing collateral materials provided an appropriate source for the photo indications used in this design for an annual report.
(Paige Johnson Design)

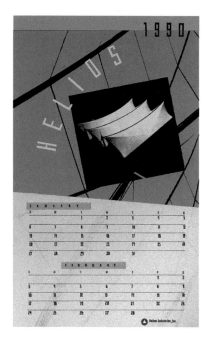

The client provided color
photographs for use as reference
for these calendar comps so that
the designer had specific images
to work with throughout the
design process. For comping,
color photocopies of the photographs were combined with
cut paper and painted elements.
(Russell Leong Design)

—COLOR PHOTOCOPIES OF EXISTING PHOTOGRAPHS. Color photocopiers can make a print from a color photo collage, an existing photograph, or a color slide. A color photocopier can also make a color print of a black-and-white photograph, in which the black is replaced by a color. Pencils and markers can be used to touch up small areas and to adjust value and hue. Although the surface of the color photocopy does not accept pencil and marker well in areas where the toner is solid, pencil and marker can be used with relative ease on areas that have less toner. You may want to feed your favorite marker or layout paper through the copier instead of the standard white bond paper provided by copy centers, in order to better anticipate how your pencils and markers will react.

—SCANS AND COMPUTER COLLAGES. If you have access to a high-resolution, black-and-white scanner, you may wish to scan your photographs into the computer, modify them, then add color appropriately. Software such as PhotoShop and Pixel Paint will allow you to modify scans. Color images can be printed out on a color printer, reproduced photographically. Check with your local service bureau to find out what is available for the software and hardware you are using.

—SHOOTING YOUR OWN PHOTOGRAPHS. When the specific subject you want to show is not available, and you have appropriate experience and equipment, consider taking slides or instant prints that show the subject. You can also "sketch" with a camera, shooting different angles and combinations of elements; this technique helps you think through and preview what you want in a photograph, while providing images for photo collages. Slides and prints can be easily converted to color photocopies, modified, and combined with other photography. This should not be thought of as a substitute for hiring a professional photographer, but may help you better understand and anticipate some of the problems the photographer will confront.

MICHAEL JAY

Once the photo shoot was complete, this image was scanned so that it could be resized and cropped easily for use in comping.

When working with color, it is easy to lose sight of the fact that you are comping, not creating art. In choosing the color materials you will be working with, keep printing limitations in mind; for example, surface influences color—ink printed on uncoated paper is perceived as being a different color than the same ink printed on coated paper. (This difference in color is so significant that PMS swatchbooks specify *U* after the PMS number for uncoated, and *C* for coated.) Color on glossy paper tends to appear darker and more saturated than color on dull paper. Although it is not possible to accurately represent every surface difference, you should be aware of how much difference the surface makes and match color accordingly.

—COLOR FIELDS. When you are showing more than one color *field* (area) keep in mind that these colors are indicating printing on white stock. (If this is not the case, make sure that no white appears in any other element on your comp.) If the colors you are showing are intended to imply tints of color, use solid colors to match what the eye would see—do not use dot screens, even though these will be used in the camera-ready art to create the tint color on the printed piece.

Pantone papers represent color fields printed in solid PMS colors, either on coated or uncoated stock. Use the paper that most clearly represents the paper you will be printing on. Keep in mind that varnishes on uncoated stock do not create a shiny surface, so when you combine coated and uncoated papers on a comp you are representing printing on a dull-coated surface and spot varnishing for the gloss, or printing on a gloss-coated surface and spot varnishing for the matte areas. When you are representing color fields that are the result of process color tints, many of the Pantone colors are inappropriate because they cannot be achieved.

Although the same Pantone colors were used in these two paper assemblies, they appear to be different because one represents printing on coated paper (left), and the other represents printing on uncoated paper (right).

This opens up the field to papers created for purposes other than comping—wrapping paper, for example, may have just the color you want. Avoid papers with a noticeable texture unless you mean to imply that the texture will appear on the printed piece. When you select your papers, use a color reference that shows combinations of process tints and match the color you see printed as closely as possible.

In working with Pantone coated paper, you may find that the protective backing is often a hindrance; for example, it is opaque on the lightbox. The adhesive may be a hindrance as well, sticking either too well or not well enough to the surface to which you are applying it. A way to avoid these problems is to cut the paper a little larger than the piece you will be using, then peel off the protective backing and stick the paper onto a sheet of tracing paper. This can then be used just as papers with no adhesive backing are used.

—WORKING WITH FILMS. Adhesive-backed films have slightly different surfaces and quite different adhesives. The stronger the adhesive, the more likely that air bubbles will be trapped beneath the film when it is applied. Air bubbles change the color of the film slightly and appear as lighter spots. Dust and particles trapped under the film not only appear as darker spots, but trap air as well. To avoid particles, brush the surface of the paper to which you are applying the film; to avoid air bubbles, apply the film from one edge, lightly rubbing it down as it makes contact with the paper. Despite these precautions, the surface still may not be perfect. When you are applying film to modify a color or to adjust the overall color of a photo indication, you need to remove the film from its backing. When you are using the film to indicate a spot varnish or an accent color, however, it may be just as easy to leave the film on the backing sheet and work with it as paper, applying spray adhesive to the back of the backing sheet to hold it in position. Leaving it on the backing sheet also makes the film opaque, indicating color printed on white. This is useful when you are placing it on a colored field.

—GRADUATED COLOR. A *gradation* is typically has value gradation from a solid color to white but can also gradate from one hue to another. The rainbow-colored gradations popular in the 1970s were often produced by putting different colors of ink in the same printing position (font) on the press; this method is called *split-font printing*. Graduated colors can be indicated by the graduated papers and films made by Pantone, if they change value within the distance you wish to indicate on your comp. If they do not, however, you can indicate gradations in a number of other ways. The most potentially time-consuming way to indicate a gradation is with an airbrush, but if the graduated papers available are not suitable, this may be the only way to achieve an even progression in value and the only way to achieve a change in hue. Tint paper with the airbrush and then trim it for use on your comp. You do not necessarily need to begin with white paper. If a gradation is yellow in the center and fades to orange at one end and green at the other, for example, you should begin with a light-yellow, uncoated Pantone paper. If the colors are dull or muted, you can get the kind of color you want by beginning with a light or medium gray. If the area is relatively small, you can use a marker sprayer instead of an airbrush. If you are handy with colored pencil and the paper surface accepts pencil well, you can also show a small graduated area on the comp by lightly sketching. This is likely to produce a texture, however that may or may not be part of what you intend to indicate in your design.

When an area on the comp fades into the background color, you may need to mask it with frisket or Magic Plus tape and color the comp surface itself to avoid a patched look. Rules and bars that blend from one hue to another can be created on separate paper using a marker sprayer, colored markers, or colored pencils. Color an area wider than the bar or rule, then trim it to size and stick it on the comp with spray adhesive.

—BLEEDS. A *bleed* is a printed element that goes all the way to the edge of the paper. When you are indicating a bleed, such as a color bar that touches the top and bottom of a page, leave the colored paper or film oversized and do not trim it until you have completed assembling your comp.

—COLOR BORDERS. If you have a color border around an element or area, mount the piece that is to have the border onto an oversized sheet of paper or film that is the color of the border, then trim the border from the edges of the mounted piece. Make sure that your original trim is *squared* (has right angles) so that your bordered piece will be square as well.

—BUTTED COLORS. When two colors *butt* (meet side by side), it is generally better to mount one color sheet on top of the other rather than to actually butt them. This will prevent any gaps caused by inexact cuts. If the butted line is not a straight line, it is especially important to layer color rather than to try to match cuts. Make sure that the lower layer is as large as the upper layer so that is not obvious where the lower layer stops.

—COLOR ACCENTS. Color is often printed as *accents*, such as bars and borders. When the accent is a bar, you can generally cut it and then place it into position. If you choose to use film, it is better to cut it in place—it is generally more difficult to align and place a rectangular strip of film than to simply cut it in place. When an accent line is very thin, such as a hairline or fine rule, one of the easiest ways to indicate it is with a ruling pen and paint (see section 3). When very small areas of color are needed and the appropriate paper or film is not at hand, you can mix and paint the color onto a piece of smooth paper, such as ledger paper, or onto treated acetate. Make sure that the painted surface is smooth and free of brushstrokes and that the paint is applied evenly so there are no variations in value. Paint a much larger area than you will need and cut a smaller area from within it so that the part you use has little or no buckling and warping.

Small detail elements, such as small squares, can be cut from paper and applied, or cut from film, but a small surface does not offer much adhesive area. Such elements are easily pushed out of position or knocked off the comp altogether. To avoid this, cut holes in the background and mount the piece onto a larger sheet that is the color of the accents. If several colors appear as accents, you can color specific areas on the backing sheet so they align with the holes. Use paint, marker, or adhesive-backed film. When you cut, work with an underlay rather than drawing directly on the comping surface, using a lightbox. Another method is to spray-mount the underlay to the back of the paper to be cut and cut from the back, following the guidelines of the underlay.

The very small, precise color details on this comp were cut as holes in the background color and laminated to the accent color rather than cut and positioned one by one. *(Randy Moravec Design)*

ILLUSTRATIONS

Comping an illustration may be one of most challenging parts of a comp, unless the illustration already exists. Just as with photo comps, color, composition, value, and overall character are at least as important as subject matter. Existing illustrations can be photocopied either in black and white or in color; line illustrations can also be resized and can be converted to transfers. If the illustration does not exist, however, the designer is faced with the task of creating something on the comp that has the same visual character and appeal as a final, professional illustration. When illustration is a dominant element in the design, it is often advisable to choose the illustrator first and include him or her in the comping process.

—ILLUSTRATION STYLE. There are a wide variety of illustration styles—illustrators use line and color in many different ways. Illustrators often advertise their skills through direct mail, and their advertisements provide a good resource for choosing style. Many illustrators also advertise in collections such as *The Workbook* and *American Showcase Illustration*; illustration annuals are another good reference for illustration styles. Seeing the styles available will help you choose an appropriate comping technique.

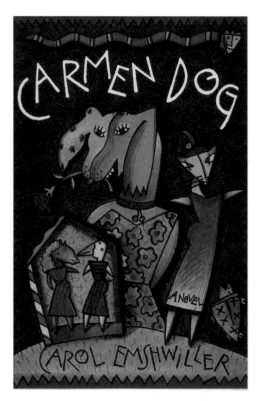

Because the illustration (left) was the dominant element for this book cover, the illustrator worked it out in great detail with the art director in sketch form first (above). The illustration became a point of departure for the rest of the design. *(Renée Flower)*

—FOUND ILLUSTRATIONS. On occasion, the designer
will find an existing illustration with a subject and style
perfectly suited to the design. Even if the subject is
only similar (e.g., a portrait of an actor to represent a
portrait of a bank president), it may suffice. A found
illustration can also act as a point of departure, to be
modified slightly—in terms of proportion, color, or the
amount of background detail, for example—or to be
used as an underlay for a very tight illustration indication. Avoid using "clip art" (copyright-free illustrations
generally used in low-budget pieces, such as grocery
store ads in the newspaper) and other such art that has
a characteristic, telltale look of generic art, unless you
are specifically trying to capture this in your design.

—INDICATED ILLUSTRATIONS. The designer should
not use a tight indication technique unless he or she
has good drawing skills. An illustration indication can
be extremely time consuming—the designer may find
that he or she has become the illustrator by default,
and this may not be the best use of the designer's time
or skills.

—LOGOS. Most corporations have camera-ready sheets
of their logos in various sizes (*slicks*) for use in printed
pieces. Many have guidelines that dictate specific ways
in which these can be used, and the designer should
ask about use restrictions pertaining to size, color, and
position on the specific printed piece being designed.
When the company cannot provide slicks, the designer
often needs to use the logo that appears on a business
card, letterhead, or other printed piece. Some logos are
simple enough to indicate. If indication is not appropriate, the logo provided should be converted to a black-
and-white master and either photocopied into position
or made into a custom transfer in the appropriate color.

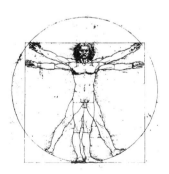

Out-of-copyright
illustrations are handy
place-holders to indi-
cate illustrations in
comps.

—EMBOSSING. To lend the proper level of realism to a comp, an embossing should actually be embossed. This will require that the designer make an embossing die or have one made by an engraver (see section 3). If the shape is a common one, such as a circle, the designer can use a drawing template as a die. Once the die is cut, embossing should always be done from the back—during the embossing process, the area of the paper being stretched along the edge of the die becomes shiny, which distracts from the overall effect, particularly for a blind embossing. Lay the embossing die face down, preferably on a lightbox, lay the paper to be embossed face down on top of the die in the appropriate position, then firmly but carefully begin to press the paper against the edges of the die with a spoon-tipped burnisher. Make two or three passes along the edge rather than trying to stretch the fibers all at once. You only need to stretch the paper along the edges of the die—do not rub the entire surface. If the die is extremely intricate, you may need to use a finer burnishing tool, but it should not be so sharp as to tear the paper fibers. Found objects, such as a manicure tip or a dried-out ball-point pen, often work well as embossing tools.

—REGISTER EMBOSSING. An easy way to create a register embossing is to use the embossing die as a spray mask. Lightly mist some spray adhesive onto the back of the embossing die and let it dry thoroughly; this will provide just enough tack to keep it in place when you spray color on the paper with a marker sprayer or airbrush. Lay the comp paper face up, then lay the embossing die in position on top of it, also face up. Tape paper to the edges of the embossing die so that the entire comp is masked before you spray. Spray the area to be colored; let the color dry thoroughly. Remove the paper being used as a mask; turn the die and comp paper face down without removing the die and emboss as described above. Remove the embossing die. One of the things many designers notice at once is that the embossing does not show up as well in a register embossing as it does in a blind embossing.

It may be more efficient to have a magnesium embossing die made for use on the comp than to cut one by hand. *(Ed Seubert)*

—FOIL STAMPING. The Color Tag system by Letraset was designed to show foil stamping. It works very well for metallic foils; nonmetallic foils work only with some paper surfaces. Because the Color Tag system bakes foil onto photocopy or laser print toner areas, you will need to photocopy or print onto the comping paper first. Another approach is to cut thin metallic papers and spray-mount them onto the comp. If you are showing a nonmetallic foil, capture its key characteristic—for example, white foil stamping looks very similar to white transfer lettering; white foil shapes can be represented by opaque white, adhesive-back film or white vinyl sign material. Zipatone makes some excellent shiny opaque films. Some foils tint the paper and make a subtle change in the paper surface; these can be represented by masking and lightly spraying color in the appropriate shape, then removing the mask and covering the shape itself with a gloss or matte frisket to indicate the plastic "foil."

Once all the elements have been created, it is time to assemble the final comp. If you have planned your comp in advance, only elements with a visible edge will need to be added—other elements, such as text, will already be in place. Assemble from small to large; for example, if your comp includes a photo with a colored border, mount the photo on a sheet of color, trim to the correct border width, then mount the subassembly onto the comp.

—ADHESIVE. The single best way to adhere elements to the comp is with spray adhesive. SprayMount, or an equivalent adhesive that is repositionable, is best because it lets you correct mistakes or change your mind. If you want to avoid using aerosols, rubber cement is the next best alternative. This often stains comping papers, so apply it evenly to the backs of surfaces rather than to the face of the comp. Make sure you apply the cement completely to corners and edges so the element doesn't curl or lift off later.

—TRIMMING. Trim the edges that are on the comp to size, but leave edges with bleeds untrimmed until the comp is entirely assembled. If possible, assemble the comp on a lightbox so that positioning guides can be on an underlay. MagicPlus tape can be placed in position and elements aligned to the edge of the tape; this is preferable to drawing lines, because it is cleaner and easier to remove MagicPlus tape than to take the chance of damaging the comp surface in erasing drawn lines. Only after everything is positioned should the final edges be trimmed.

—STORAGE BEFORE MOUNTING. If a number of comps are being assembled at once, keep them in a folder and separate them with tracing paper, so that delicate surfaces do not get scratched and edges do not get chipped or bent.

—MOUNTING. Most comps are presented on black or neutral gray mounting board. It is most common to use 16-by-20-inch board unless the comp is quite large. Mount the comp only after it has been trimmed. Center it left and right, but leave a little more space below the comp than above it—if the same amount of space appears below as above, the comp will look as though it is below center. Avoid positioning the comp asymmetrically—you do not want the position on the mounting board to distract from the comp itself or become part of the design.

An assemblage of elements created in the comping stage of this project was modified and used for color separating (left). The black detail was shot separately to keep it crisp (center). The printed piece (right) retains the qualities of the papers used in the original comp. The number 50 is foil embossing, and was added after printing.
(Mark Anderson Design)

Designers working on the screen can apply many of the strategies used for producing paper comps, because they have similar objectives. There is as much difference between sketches and comps on the screen as between sketches and comps on paper—the designer is confronting the same visualization and communication problems. Working with a paint program or drawing software is much like sketching on marker or tracing paper, whereas creating elements in several programs and then integrating these using a layout program is much like the assembly technique in comps in which refined elements are assembled into a comp.

—BRIDGING TO PRODUCTION. Coordination between comping and production is becoming more common; for example, the color separator can scan key photographs and then provide the designer with comp-quality scans to use for layout and positioning. These scans can be cropped, scaled, and otherwise manipulated in the comp; the position scans are replaced by production-quality scans by the color separator. Once a computer-based comp is approved, text can replace greeking. A file generated for the comp, then, may undergo relatively little change to become a file for production art.

The closer the connection between the comp and production, the more planning and preparation will need to be done before the comp is produced and the less work will need to be done after the comp has been produced. In evaluating the relative cost between computer comps and paper comps, production costs become a significant factor.

The folds and artwork on this accordion-folded new year's card (far right) needed to align precisely. All of the sketches and comps were done on the computer; once the design was worked out (right), no more work was necessary to convert this to camera-ready art. *(West and Moravec)*

—PLANNING a computer-based comp is much like planning a comp made of paper—both require carefully detailed thumbnails and will require that all of the elements be created or assembled before you begin. You will also need to plan the tools and strategies you will use. Part of planning is considering presentation. If slides will be made at a service center, you will need to determine the size and proportions that will fit on a slide, and confirm that the software you are planning to use is compatible with the slide-making equipment available. If you are shooting slides directly from the screen, you will not be able to work actual size unless the screen is large enough to accommodate the image. Keep in mind that screens and slides have considerably different proportions—because the screen is more square, if the entire width of the screen is on the slide the top and bottom of the screen will be truncated.

If you are presenting on screen, scale and proportion are critical—you will want the entire layout to appear on the screen. Once you have completed working on the comp, resave your file as a presentation file, and set it up with a minimum of software paraphernalia showing—toolboxes and other extraneous elements should be hidden; the background should be a dark, neutral color such as black. Decide on a labeling strategy if multiple screens will be shown, and be consistent from screen to screen.

—PRINTOUTS. Even if you present comps on slides or on the screen, it is often useful to have hard-copy printouts that can be seen simultaneously and discussed after the presentation. Although these may not be comp quality and may have some color variations, they are invaluable as reference. Because color changes so much from technology to technology, be prepared to create a second version of your file in which you adjust the color so that you get the best print results.

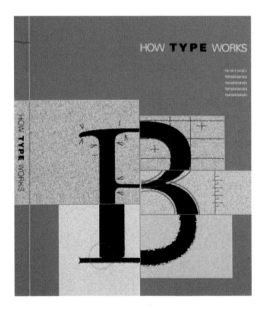

These screen sketches for a typography book cover were developed in PhotoShop, and were originally presented on screen.
(Randy Moravec Design)

Photographic prints are a good alternative to printouts from color printers because photographic color is likely to look more like the screen. If the software you are using can create color overlays, the overlays can be run out as film negatives and the negatives can be used to make a Color Key or Cromatec color proof. Although these are generally used only for proofing negatives for printing, the system works well on jobs with generous budgets.

—COMPS OF SYMBOLS AND LOGOS. It is often effective to present a sequence, either on screen or slides, showing not only the black-and-white version of the symbol but also how it looks reversed, in different scales, in different colors and color combinations, and perhaps even how the symbol looks applied. If it is a logo, for example, it can be shown on a building sign, a business card, or other typical application. If the symbol will be appearing on screen as well as in print, showing the symbol in a small size on screen will show how well the symbol adapts to low-resolution digital technology. Once a design has been approved, the transition to production art is remarkably fast; only minor modifications may be needed to make the transition from comp to production art.

Data sheet variations were designed completely on screen in PhotoShop and presented to the client on screen. The thumbnails above were the only notes made on paper before the designer began working on the computer. *(Randy Moravec Design)*

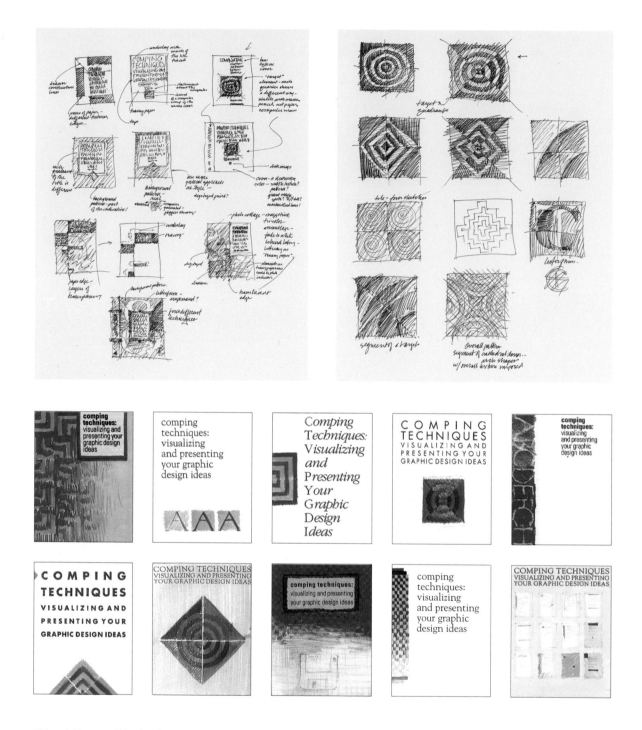

Although ideas would be developed using a computer, initial thumbnails were drawn conventionally (top left). Specific graphic element were explored as loose sketches (top right).

Using the thumbnails as a point of departure, additional sketching was done in a layout program (bottom rows). Type was printed directly on tracing paper; graphic elements were printed separately as underlays.

Some of the same ideas were resketched and refined in a color paint program so that variations in sizes, colors, and positions of elements could be explored. Because different mediums inspire different ideas, additional ideas were also explored. The screen sketches were shot as slides for a preliminary presentation.

After a design direction was chosen, conventional paper comps were created (below). The background patterns are color printouts; type was set in a layout program and laser printed onto sheets of acetate. Acetate and paper were spray-mounted to the printouts.

In the appendix you will find disk information; type specimens to use for reference and as underlays; comparison charts for sketching and comping on paper and on screen; and grids in several sizes to use as underlays.

The type specimens provided here can be used as underlays for sketching. They are arranged head-to-head to make sketching easier. You can also photocopy text blocks to use as greeking on a comping master. The typefaces and sizes provided here give an idea of the range of styles, textures, and colors of type and how these factors influence the look of a layout. If you are working with a computer but are more comfortable comping on paper, you may want to make some type specimen sheets of your own.

Two grids have been included; each is shown in three sizes. The reduce grids are useful as underlays for sketching; the full-sized grids are useful as layout guides and for creating comping masters. You may wish to compile a wider array of grids to use as reference when comping; begin with the additional grids provided on the disk. You can "reverse-engineer" grids by drawing lines where you see elements aligning in your favorite magazine or printed piece. Plan to study multiple pages to find the entire grid. (Keep in mind that grids are not always followed exactly.)

The comparison charts list common printing effects or techniques and how to indicate and comp them, both on paper and on the screen. Use these charts as a point of departure; as you comp, you may discover additional techniques. If you aren't familiar with prepress and printing, read the background information in section 1 to put this chart in context.

A disk is provided in the back of this book. It contains files to use as a point of departure for comping. Some of the files, such as the greeking files, will be handy to use in layout comps. Others are provided as examples, models, and points of departure for those just beginning to use the Macintosh as a comping and designing tool. A number of different software programs were used to create these files; although you may not have all of the software to open and use all of the files provided, you will be able to work with many of them if you have any current graphic application software and a Macintosh computer.

There are two ways to open files, from the finder and from within an application. If the software you are using is similar to the software used to create a file, you may be able to open that file by opening your application first. For example, the greeking and the *Read Me* files are word processing files created in MacWrite. Even if you do not have MacWrite, you can open these files from within another word processing program. You also have access to these files from layout programs that allow you to import text files.

The *Read Me* file has more information about the files on the disk. Be sure to print it out and read it before beginning to work. In the process of doing this, you will also be testing for system compatibility.

ABCDEFGHIJKLMN
OPQRSTUVWXYZ&
1234567890?/!abc
defghijklmnopqrst
uvwxyz

ABCDEFGHIJKLM
NOPQRSTUVWXY
Z&1234567890?/!
abcdefghijklmnop
qrstuvwxyz

Many of the tasks assumed by the graphic designer today were done by the typesetter or the commercial artist only a few decades ago. The materials and tools used by the commercial artist were the same as those used by the fine artist, and many of the same skills were required. Lettering was an essential skill, as were basic drawing and painting. New tools and materials change the specific skills required to visualize ideas. The commercial artist relied on lettering and drawing skills; the graphic designer relies on sketching and assembly techniques; basic computer skills and procedures shift the emphasis yet again. What remains consistent is the process of design itself. (9/11)

Many of the tasks assumed by the graphic designer today were done by the typesetter or the commercial artist only a few decades ago. The materials and tools used by the commercial artist were the same as those used by the fine artist, and many of the same skills were required. Lettering was an essential skill, as were basic drawing and painting. New tools and materials change the specific skills required to visualize ideas. The commercial artist relied on lettering and drawing skills; the graphic designer relies on sketching and assembly techniques; basic computer skills and procedures shift the emphasis yet again.

What remains consistent is the process of design itself. (8/15)

ABCDEFGHIJKLMNOP
QRSTUVWXYZ&12345
67890?/!abcdefghijklm
nopqrstuvwxyz

ABCDEFGHIJKLM
NOPQRSTUVWXY
Z&1234567890?/!
abcdefghijklmnop
qrstuvwxyz

Many of the tasks assumed by the graphic designer today were done by the typesetter or the
commercial artist only a few decades ago. The
materials and tools used by the commercial artist
were the same as those used by the fine artist,
and many of the same skills were required. Lettering was an essential skill, as were basic drawing
and painting. New tools and materials change the
specific skills required to visualize ideas. The
commercial artist relied on lettering and drawing
skills; the graphic designer relies on sketching and
assembly techniques; basic computer skills and
procedures shift the emphasis yet again. What
remains consistent is the process of design itself.
(9/11)

Many of the tasks assumed by the graphic designer
today were done by the typesetter or the commercial
artist only a few decades ago. The materials and tools
used by the commercial artist were the same as those
used by the fine artist, and many of the same skills were
required. Lettering was an essential skill, as were basic
drawing and painting. New tools and materials change
the specific skills required to visualize ideas. The commercial artist relied on lettering and drawing skills; the
graphic designer relies on sketching and assembly techniques; basic computer skills and procedures shift the
emphasis yet again. What remains consistent is the
process of design itself. (8/15)

ABCDEFGHIJKLMNOPQR STUVWXYZ&1234567890?! /!abcdefghijklmnopqrstu

VWXYZ

ABCDEFGHIJK LMNOPQRSTU VWXYZ&12345 67890?/!abcdef ghijklmnopqrst uvwxyz

Many of the tasks assumed by the graphic designer today were done by the typesetter or the commercial artist only a few decades ago. The materials and tools used by the commercial artist were the same as those used by the fine artist, and many of the same skills were required. Lettering was an essential skill, as were basic drawing and painting. New tools and materials change the specific skills required to visualize ideas. The commercial artist relied on lettering and drawing skills; the graphic designer relies on sketching and assembly techniques; basic computer skills and procedures shift the emphasis yet again. What remains consistent is the process of design itself. (7/14)

Many of the tasks assumed by the graphic designer today were done by the typesetter or the commercial artist only a few decades ago. The materials and tools used by the commercial artist were the same as those used by the fine artist, and many of the same skills were required. Lettering was an essential skill, as were basic drawing and painting. New tools and materials change the specific skills required to visualize ideas. The commercial artist relied on lettering and drawing skills; the graphic designer relies on sketching and assembly techniques; basic computer skills and procedures shift the emphasis yet again. What remains consistent is the process of design itself. (10/13)

Many of the tasks assumed by the graphic designer today were done by the typesetter or the commercial artist only a few decades ago. The materials and tools used by the commercial artist were the same as those used by the fine artist, and many of the same skills were required. Lettering was an essential skill, as were basic drawing and painting. New tools and materials change the specific skills required to visualize ideas. The commercial artist relied on lettering and drawing skills; the graphic designer relies on sketching and assembly techniques; basic computer skills and procedures shift the emphasis yet again. What remains consistent is the process of design itself. (9/15)

ABCDEFGHIJKLMNOPQRST
UVWXYZ&1234567890?/!a
bcdefghijklmnopqrstuvwxyz

ABCDEFGHIJKL
MNOPQRSTUV
WXYZ&123456
7890?/!abcdef
ghijklmnopqrst
uvwxyz

Many of the tasks assumed by the graphic designer today were done by the typesetter or the commercial artist only a few decades ago. The materials and tools used by the commercial artist were the same as those used by the fine artist, and many of the same skills were required. Lettering was an essential skill, as were basic drawing and painting. New tools and materials change the specific skills required to visualize ideas. The commercial artist relied on lettering and drawing skills; the graphic designer relies on sketching and assembly techniques; basic computer skills and procedures shift the emphasis yet again. What remains consistent is the process of design itself. (9/15)

Many of the tasks assumed by the graphic designer today were done by the typesetter or the commercial artist only a few decades ago. The materials and tools used by the commercial artist were the same as those used by the fine artist, and many of the same skills were required. Lettering was an essential skill, as were basic drawing and painting. New tools and materials change the specific skills required to visualize ideas. The commercial artist relied on lettering and drawing skills; the graphic designer relies on sketching and assembly techniques; basic computer skills and procedures shift the emphasis yet again. What remains consistent is the process of design itself. (9/11)

Many of the tasks assumed by the graphic designer today were done by the typesetter or the commercial artist only a few decades ago. The materials and tools used by the commercial artist were the same as those used by the fine artist, and many of the same skills were required. Lettering was an essential skill, as were basic drawing and painting. New tools and materials change the specific skills required to visualize ideas. The commercial artist relied on lettering and drawing skills; the graphic designer relies on sketching and assembly techniques; basic computer skills and procedures shift the emphasis yet again. What remains consistent is the process of design itself. (7/14)

ABCDEFGHIJKLMNOP
QRSTUVWXYZ&12345
67890?!◆!abcdefghijklmno
pqrstuvwxyz

ABCDEFGHIJKLM
NOPQRSTUVWX
YZ&1234567890?!◆!
abcdefghijklmnopqr
stuvwxyz

Many of the tasks assumed by the graphic designer today were done by the typesetter or the commercial artist only a few decades ago. The materials and tools used by the commercial artist were the same as those used by the fine artist, and many of the same skills were required. Lettering was an essential skill, as were basic drawing and painting. New tools and materials change the specific skills required to visualize ideas. The commercial artist relied on lettering and drawing skills; the graphic designer relies on sketching and assembly techniques; basic computer skills and procedures shift the emphasis yet again. What remains consistent is the process of design itself. (9/12)

Many of the tasks assumed by the graphic designer today were done by the typesetter or the commercial artist only a few decades ago. The materials and tools used by the commercial artist were the same as those used by the fine artist, and many of the same skills were required. Lettering was an essential skill, as were basic drawing and painting. New tools and materials change the specific skills required to visualize ideas. The commercial artist relied on lettering and drawing skills; the graphic designer relies on sketching and assembly techniques; basic computer skills and procedures shift the emphasis yet again. What remains consistent is the process of design itself. (11/15)

ABCDEFGHIJKLMNO
PQRSTUVWXYZ& 123
4567890?!.abcdefghijkl
mnopqrstuvwxyz

Many of the tasks assumed by the graphic designer today were done by the typesetter or the commercial artist only a few decades ago. The materials and tools used by the commercial artist were the same as those used by the fine artist, and many of the same skills were required. Lettering was an essential skill, as were basic drawing and painting. New tools and materials change the specific skills required to visualize ideas. The commercial artist relied on lettering and drawing skills; the graphic designer relies on sketching and assembly techniques; basic computer skills and procedures shift the emphasis yet again. What remains consistent is the process of design itself. (11/15)

ABCDEFGHIJKLM
NOPQRSTUVWXY
Z&1234567890?!.ab
cdefghijklmnopqrst
uvwxyz

Many of the tasks assumed by the graphic designer today were done by the typesetter or the commercial artist only a few decades ago. The materials and tools used by the commercial artist were the same as those used by the fine artist, and many of the same skills were required. Lettering was an essential skill, as were basic drawing and painting. New tools and materials change the specific skills required to visualize ideas. The commercial artist relied on lettering and drawing skills; the graphic designer relies on sketching and assembly techniques; basic computer skills and assembly techniques; basic computer skills and procedures shift the emphasis yet again. What remains consistent is the process of design itself. (9/13)

COMPARISON CHART: INDICATION TECHNIQUES

PRODUCTION OR PRINTING EFFECT	INDICATION TECHNIQUES
TEXT TYPE	
Black or color on white	Marker, ink, paint, or pencil with underlay
White on black or color	White paint with ruling pen or brush with underlay
Color on darker color	Marker or pencil on colored field with underlay
Color on lighter color	Ruling pen or pencil on colored field with underlay
DISPLAY TYPE	
Black or color on white	Marker, ink, paint, or pencil with underlay
White on black or color	White paint with ruling pen or brush with underlay
Color on darker color	Marker, paint, or pencil on colored field with underlay
Color on lighter color	Paint with ruling pen or brush with underlay
PHOTOGRAPH	
Black and white	Marker and pencil with underlay
Duotone	Marker and pencil with underlay plus spray marker or pencil accent color
Color	Marker and pencil with underlay
ILLUSTRATION	
Spot line art	Marker, ink, paint, or pencil
Large line art	Marker, ink, paint, or pencil
Large continuous tone black and white	Marker and pencil
Large continuous tone color art	Marker and pencil
COLOR	
Accent color	Marker, ink, paint, or pencil
Color fields	Marker or pencil
Color detail	Painted detail over colored field with underlay
Gradated color	Pencil or spray marker with mask
PMS color match	Paint, spray marker, or marker and pencil
EMBOSSING AND DIE CUTTING	
Blind embossing	Marker or pencil shadow and highlight to define shape
Register embossing	Marker or pencil shadow and hightlight on colored shape
Die cut hole	Marker or pencil shadow and highlight with second layer indicated
Die cut outside shape; folds	Isometric sketch or 3-D mock-up with indication

COMPARISON CHART: COMPING TECHNIQUES

PRODUCTION OR PRINTING EFFECT	COMPING TECHNIQUES
TEXT TYPE	
Black on white or color	Transfer text; found text as photocopy or stat; laser-printed text
White on black or color	White transfer text; custom transfer; reverse stat; negative film
Color on darker color	Paint or marker indication; custom transfer
Color on lighter color	Paint indication; custom transfer
DISPLAY TYPE	
Black or color on white	Laser-printed type; transfer type; custom transfer
White on black or color	White transfer type; custom transfer
Color on darker color	Custom transfer; white transfer type tinted with spray marker
Color on lighter color	Custom transfer; transfer type tinted with spray marker
PHOTOGRAPH	
Black and white	Tight indication; found photograph; photocopy
Duotone	Tight indication or photocopy plus spray marker or pencil
Color	Tight indication; found photograph; color photocopy
ILLUSTRATION	
Spot line art	Tight indication; photocopy; custom transfer
Large line art	Tight indication; found illustratio; photocopy of existing illustration
Large continuous-tone black and white	Photocopy or stat of found or existing illustration
Large continuous-tone color	Color photocopy of found or existing illustration
COLOR	
Accent color	Marker, ink, paint, film, or paper
Color fields	Colored paper or film
Color detail	Marker, ink, or paint; custom transfer; colored film
Gradated color	Gradated paper or film; spray marker with mask
PMS color match	Colored paper or film; or custom transfer
EMBOSSING, DIES, AND FOLDS	
Embossing or debossing die	Cut cardboard or commercial magnesium die
Blind embossing or debossing	Emboss or deboss with die
Register embossing	Cardboard die as mask for spray marker, then emboss
Foil stamping	Custom transfer; colored paper; Color Tag on photocopy
Die cut hole	Cut in place after lamination but before assembly
Scoring	Score for folds; score to indicate a fold
Folding and trimming	Fold on scores; trim after assembly is complete
Die cut outside shape	Cut when assembly and folding are complete

PRINTING EFFECT	PROGRAM (TECHNIQUE)	OUTPUT OF SKETCH
TEXT		
Black and white	Paint or draw program	Laser-print on tracing paper
Color	Color paint program	Color printout; slide
DISPLAY TYPE		
Black and white	Paint or draw program	Laser-print on tracing paper
Color	Color paint program	Color printout; slide
PHOTOGRAPHS & ILLUSTRATIONS		
Black and white	Scan; paint program	Laser-print on tracing paper
Color	Scan (colorize); color paint program	Color printout; slide
COLOR		
Color accents and detail	Color paint program; paint program	Color printout; paint on laser printout
Color fields	Color paint program	Color printout; slide
Graduated color or split font	Color paint program	Color printout; slide
Matching an ink color	Color paint program	Color printout; slide
EMBOSSING AND DIE CUTING		
Embossing; die-cut hole	Paint or draw program	Laser printout; slide
Foil stamping	Color paint program	Color printout; slide

COMPARISON CHART: COMPUTER-BASED COMPING

PRINTING EFFECT	PROGRAM (TECHNIQUE)	OUTPUT FOR ASSEMBLY
TYPESETTING		
Black on white or color	Draw or layout program	Laser-print on white or color stock
		Image-set on film
White on black	Draw or layout program	Reverse laser printout on white
		Image-set reverse on film
Black on color	Draw or layout program	Laser-print on color stock
		Image-set on film
White on color	Draw or layout program	Laser-print reverse for color photocopy
		Image-set negative for transfers
Color on color	Draw or layout program	Laser-print for color photocopy
		Image-set negative for transfers
PHOTOGRAPHS & ILLUSTRATIONS		
Black and white	Scan	Export and combine with other elements
Spot black-and-white art	Paint program (indicate)	Export and combine with other elements
Duotone	Scan	Color photocopy of laser printout
		Add pencil to laser printout
Color	Scan (colorize)	Color printout
COLOR		
Color accent and detail	Draw or layout program	Laser-print and paint or Color Tag
		Image-set master for transfers
Color fields	Color paint program	Color printout
Graduation or split font	Color paint program	Color printout
EMBOSSING, DIES, FOLDS AND CUTS		
Embossing or debossing die	Draw or layout program	Laser-print cutting guideline
Die cut hole	Draw or layout program	Laser-print cutting guideline
Folding and trimming	Draw or layout program	Laser-print fold and crop lines
Die cut outside shape	Draw or layout program	Laser-print cutting guidelines

END USER LICENSING AGREEMENT

IMPORTANT! READ BEFORE OPENING SEALED DISKETTE

The templates in this package are provided to You on the condition that You agree with Watson-Guptill Publications, Inc. ("W-G") to the terms and conditions set forth below. Please read this End User License Agreement carefully. You will be bound by the terms of this agreement if You open the sealed diskette. If You do not agree to the terms contained in this End User License Agreement, return the entire package, along with your receipt of purchase, to Watson-Guptill, Inc., Department TM, 1695 Oak Street, Lakewood, NJ 08701, and W-G will refund your purchase price.

W-G grants, and You hereby accept, a personal, nonexclusive license to use the templates and associated documentation in this package, or any part of it ("Licensed Product"), subject to the following terms and conditions:

I. License

The license granted to You hereunder by W-G authorizes You to use the Licensed Product on any single computer system. A separate license, pursuant to a separate End User License Agreement, is required from W-G for any other computer system on which You intend to use the Licensed Product.

II. Term

This End User License Agreement between You and W-G is effective from the date of purchase of the Licensed Product by You and shall remain in force until terminated. At any time you may terminate this End User License Agreement by destroying the Licensed Product together with all copies in any form made by You or received by You. Your right to use or copy the Licensed Product will terminate if You fail to comply with any of the terms or conditions of this End User License Agreement. Upon such termination You shall destroy the copies of the Licensed Product in your possession.

III. Restrictions Against Transfer

The End User License Agreement, and the Licensed Product, may not be assigned, sublicensed, or otherwise transferred by You to another party unless the other party agrees to accept the terms and conditions of this End User License Agreement. If you transfer the Licensed Product, at the same time you must either transfer all copies whether in printed or machine-readable form to the same party or destroy any copies not transferred.

IV. Restrictions Against Copying or Modifying the Licensed Product

The Licensed Product is copyrighted and may not be further copied without the prior written approval of W-G except that You may make one copy for backup purposes provided You produce and include the complete copyright notice on the backup copy. Any unauthorized copying is in violation of this agreement and may also constitute a violation of the United States Copyright Law for which You could be liable in a civil or criminal suit. You may not use, transfer, copy or otherwise reproduce the Licensed Product, or any part of it, except as expressly permitted in this End User License Agreement.

V. Protection and Security

All reasonable steps shall be taken by You to safeguard the Licensed Product, to ensure that no unauthorized person shall have access to it, and to ensure that no unauthorized copy of any part of it in any form shall be made.

VI. Limited Warranty

If You are the original consumer purchaser of the diskette in this package and it is found to be defective in materials or workmanship (which shall not include problems relating to the nature of operation of the Licensed Product) under normal use, W-G will replace it free of charge (or, at W-G's option, refund your purchase price) within 30 days following the date of purchase. Following the 30-day period, and up to one year after purchase, W-G will replace any such defective diskette on payment of a $5 charge (or, at W-G's option, refund your purchase price), provided that any request for replacement of a defective diskette is accompanied by the original defective diskette and proof of date of purchase and purchase price. W-G shall have no obligation to replace a diskette (or refund your purchase price) based on claims of defects in the nature or operation of the Licensed Product.

The templates in this package are provided "as is" without warranty of any kind, either expressed or implied, including but not limited to the implied warranties of merchantability and fitness for a particular purpose. The entire risk as to the quality and performance of the program is with You. Should the program prove defective, You (and not W-G) assume the entire cost of all necessary servicing, repair, or correction.

Some states do not allow the exclusion of implied warranties, so the above exclusion may not apply to You. This warrant gives You specific legal rights, and You may also have other rights that vary from state to state.

W-G does not warrant that the functions contained in the program will meet your requirements or that the operation of the program will be uninterrupted or error free. Neither W-G nor anyone else who has been involved in the creation or production of this product shall be liable for any direct, indirect, incidental, special, or consequential damages, whether arising out of the use or inability to use the product, or any breach of a warranty, and W-G shall have no responsibility except to replace the diskette pursuant to this limited warranty (or at its option, provide a refund or the purchase price).

No sales personnel or other representative of any party involved in the distribution of the Licensed Product is authorized by W-G to make any warranties with respect to the diskette or the Licensed Product beyond those contained in this End User License Agreement. Oral statements do not constitute warranties, shall not be relied on by You, and are not part of this agreement. The entire agreement between W-G and You is embodied in this End User License Agreement.

VII. General

If any provision of this End User License Agreement is determined to be invalid under any applicable statutes or rule of law, it shall be deemed omitted, and the remaining provisions shall continue in full force and effect. This End User License Agreement is to be governed by and construed with the laws of the State of New York.